"A rush of water; you can see nothing but the grace of God; I must take advantage of it and examine nature carefully, for I shall never return to these waters again. Instinct tells me to let myself drift with the swift current. Reason stops me; for an explorer, hurrying through an unknown land is like running away from the enemy."

"I am sitting on my little bench, my ship's compass in front of me, my notebook on my lap. I am recording our course as we go along."

"The virgin forest – what they call 'tall timber' in Guiana – has a forbidding, cold look to it. Countless colonnades 35 or 40 metres high. From them issue the songs of birds with incomparably rich and variegated plumage."

"This band of Indians, which could have been mistaken for a moving forest, streamed alongside us at an easy trot."

"Uanica climbed up a nearby tree. He was holding a long, thin pole to which he had fastened a piece of rope, forming a noose. He slipped it around the animal's neck and gave it a sharp tug."

CONTENTS

1 CINNAMON IN THE AIR
13

2 LIVING LEGENDS
39

3 THE AGE OF REASON PENETRATES THE RAIN FOREST
59

4 THE GREAT RUBBER ADVENTURE
77

5 THE INDIAN AND THE RAIN FOREST
97

DOCUMENTS
129

Chronology
184

Further Reading
185

List of Illustrations
186

Index
189

THE AMAZON
PAST, PRESENT AND FUTURE

Alain Gheerbrant

THAMES AND HUDSON

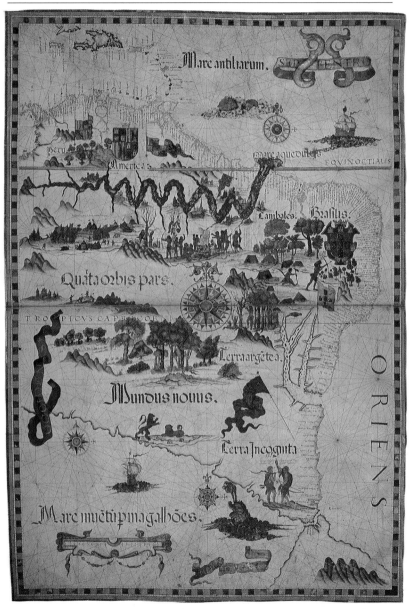

"Why did the Indians defend themselves in this manner? ...they are the subjects of...the Amazons, and, our coming having been made known to them, they had gone to them for help.... We saw the Amazons in front of all the Indian men as women captains, fighting so courageously that the Indians did not dare to turn their backs, and if they did the women clubbed them to death before our very eyes."

Gaspar de Carvajal

CHAPTER 1
CINNAMON IN
THE AIR

"With eyes wide open, the conquistadors lived in a lucid and endless delirium."
Jean Descola

Although Vicente Yáñez Pinzón (who had commanded the *Niña* on Christopher Columbus' first voyage) first sighted the Amazon delta in 1500, the discovery of the land beyond it, which came to be known as the 'Green Hell', did not begin for another forty years. And it came not from the Atlantic, but from the lonely glare of the Andean altiplano, an

unforgiving land conducive to migrations, mirages and dreams.

After a perilous journey, Gonzalo Pizarro reaches Quito on 1 December 1540

Two hundred Spaniards, half of them on horseback, accompanied Pizarro as he set out from the Peruvian capital of Cuzco with orders from his older brother, the conquistador

The conquistador Francisco Pizarro (left).

Francisco, to take over as *gobernador* of Quito, about 1600 kilometres to the north. Their ranks were bound to thin along the way; so when he found his cousin, the brilliant lieutenant-general Francisco de Orellana, founder of Guayaquil, welcoming him at the city gates and putting himself at his disposal, a heartened Gonzalo was quick to accept his offer.

Orellana knew full well that this administrative shuffle – the naming of a new governor – was, in fact, a pretext for an altogether different mission so ambitious and thrilling that he insisted on joining up. So the two men struck a bargain. Orellana would head back to Guayaquil to muster all available manpower and equipment. Gonzalo would take office in Quito, make preparations for the coming campaign and wait for his cousin to return.

They both came from Trujillo in Extremadura, Spain, as did Balboa, Cortés, the other Pizarros and

many other conquistadors. Seasoned campaigners by the age of thirty, they had weathered many an ordeal since the conquest of Peru had begun, seven years earlier. But neither had any inkling of the strange turn of events that awaited them during their next adventure.

An imposing barrier of perpetual snow looms east of Quito: what lies beyond?

Cinnamon – at least that was the rumour. Open country carpeted with cinnamon! In an age when spices were as alluring as gold, there was

Fifty-three of the loftiest volcanic peaks in the Andes rise above the altiplano of Quito on one side and foothills sloping down to the Amazon on the other.

Spices, valued not only for their culinary applications, but for medicinal properties we are only now starting to rediscover, played an unexpectedly pivotal role in the exploration of the world. Cinnamon is an antiseptic, a powerful digestive and a respiratory stimulant.

magic in the word. Hadn't Columbus himself sought a cinnamon route? Who could tell – this scent just might lead to El Dorado!

It took Pizarro less than three months to prepare. An acting governor of Quito took office on 18 February 1541. With no sign of Orellana, three days later Pizarro decided to leave without him.

The procession that marched out on 21 February onto the Andean altiplano and towards the peaks of the Cordillera was an unbelievable spectacle. Leading it were three hundred and fifty armoured *hidalgos* (two hundred of them on horseback), followed by two thousand ferocious dogs trained to attack Indians, and four thousand 'volunteer' porters (conscripted Indians) laden with weapons, provisions and, to quote 16th-century chronicler Garcilaso de la Vega, 'iron, axes, hatchets, hemp ropes and nails'. Next came two thousand similarly burdened llamas, and two thousand pigs brought up the rear. The Spaniards marched into the Cordillera each carrying nothing more than a sword, a small shield and a supply kit. The weather deteriorated; they were pelted by torrential rain, driven by the

Peru was the source of a river of gold that in less than twenty years washed over Europe and had even upset its geopolitical balance. The river began in the Andes, where jewelry, sacred vessels and sculpture snatched from Inca temples were melted down to ingots in compact Spanish-built furnaces. From there commandeered llamas transported the treasure-turned-commodity down to the coast, where the gold bars were then loaded into galleons.

Crossing the Andes.

wind. Horses slipped on the snow-covered rock, the column slowed and Indians started collapsing. This first ordeal alone claimed a hundred of them. Then came forests so dense that their only path was the one they themselves hacked out, metre by metre, with axes and machetes.

Meanwhile, Orellana had set out behind them and was advancing by forced march. Although less encumbered and therefore more mobile, he was harried by bands of Indians. By the time he finally caught up with Pizarro a month later, he had lost all his horses and gear. His twenty-one surviving men carried nothing but their swords. The journey thus far had been so gruelling for all concerned that they had travelled only thirty leagues (about 150 kilometres) from Quito, although Pizarro thought it was sixty.

Pizarro decided to explore ahead with a small party, leaving the main

Gold fever and the allure of spices inspired unreasoning greed in Spanish soldiers and turned these rugged sons of a stinting land into ruthless conquerors.

Indians not already cowed by the Spaniards' horses were utterly terrified of their specially trained dogs. Pizarro brought two thousand ferocious Indian-attacking dogs on his expedition (left).

body of the expedition with Orellana. Seventy days later he finally reached what he hoped would be the Promised Land. And he did indeed find cinnamon trees, but they were so few and so scattered they could not be farmed commercially.

So keen was Pizarro's disappointment that he threw half of his guides to the dogs and burned the other half alive. He and his party then headed north, discovered a 'fair river', met up with some peaceable Indians, and promptly made off with sixteen of their canoes.

After Orellana and the other men caught up with him, they all laboured along the banks of this river for about 100 km until it emptied into a much larger waterway 'half a league wide', according to the expedition's chronicler, Dominican friar Gaspar de Carvajal. At this juncture Pizarro decided to stop long enough to build a brigantine. The boat could just accommodate twenty or so

passengers, and into it were crammed all the heavy equipment and the ailing remnants of the four thousand 'volunteers' recruited in Quito. The name of the village that now stands at this site, near the confluence of the Coca and the Napo rivers in Ecuador, is El Barco – a reminder of their ship.

The expeditioners started out again, most of them trudging along on foot since they had only the sixteen canoes in addition to their little brig. Fresh hardships awaited them. They had to manoeuvre around marshes and improvise bridges, and provisions were running low. Before long they had slaughtered the last of the pigs. After about three hundred kilometres, morale flagged.

Since they had been told that in just a few days they would reach prosperous villages, Orellana suggested that he take sixty men and the brigantine and canoes downstream to forage for food. Pizarro acquiesced, and Orellana set off. It was 26 December 1541 – a day Pizarro would come to rue, for he never saw Orellana or his shipmates again.

Once Pizarro and his men had eaten the last of the dogs and remaining hundred horses, they had to turn back, embittered and enraged at Orellana's

In the 16th century explorers looked upon Amazonian Indians as neither 'noble savages' nor ferocious headhunters. Acknowledging their humanity, the conquistadors called attention to those differences that accounted for (though did not excuse) the natives' ignorance of the True Faith. Engravings from the time reflect the Spaniards' attitude.

presumed treachery. It took them six months to struggle back overland to Quito. It took Orellana only
slightly longer to discover the mightiest river on earth.

'I celebrated Mass, as is customary at sea, to commend our souls and lives to God'

Gaspar de Carvajal was among Orellana's contingent
and kept a detailed diary of the expedition. 'The
current was so strong,' he notes, 'that we covered
twenty-five leagues [approximately 120 kilometres] a
day from the very start, and it would have been all but
impossible to sail back against it.' What is more, the
prosperous villages they had been promised did not
materialize. They were forced to press on.

One long week later the Spaniards finally heard the
sound of drums beating in the jungle, and a village
came into view. Orellana presented the local chieftain,
Aparia, with some purple clothes and promptly
pronounced him a subject of Emperor Charles V, in
whose name he officially took possession of the
chieftain's domain. Orellana christened this the 'land
of Aparia the Lesser', for he soon learned that
downriver there lived another Aparia, a far more
important overlord whom he called Aparia the Great.

The detachment deliberated on the promise they
had made to Pizarro. They all agreed that it was
virtually impossible to labour back up the 1200 km
of raging river they had just negotiated. It would be
better to keep going and make their way back to Peru
by sea, which, judging by the river's steadily increasing
width, they felt could not be far off.

Since canoes would hardly do for an ocean voyage,
Orellana concluded that a second brigantine had
to be built. Rough soldiers turned into
impromptu woodcutters and charcoal makers;
the hardest part was forging the two thousand
nails they would need. A month went by, and
relations with the Indians began to sour. Orellana
decided it was time to move on; besides, there would
be plenty of time to assemble the boat downriver.

The anonymous 19th-
century artist who
drew these Indians called
them Napo after the river
along which they lived.
They belong to the Shuar
nation – better known as
the Jívaro – of
Ecuadorian Amazonia.

Before setting out again, however, the shrewd leader contrived to get himself unanimously elected captain-general and representative of the Spanish crown in Gonzalo Pizarro's stead. A document to that effect was drawn up, countersigned by the entire contingent and duly witnessed by a scrivener. Whereupon Orellana offered a thousand castillanos – equal to about four kilos of gold – to any six men willing to go back and take the news to Pizarro. Only three volunteered. Given the ordeals they were bound to face, they would not be enough. The idea was dropped. The expedition struck out again.

The Indian groups Gonzalo Pizarro, Francisco de Orellana and their men encountered from the Río Coca to the mouth of the Napo were probably all Shuar. They were famous for their practice of shrinking trophy heads.

On 11 February 1542 they unknowingly sail out of the Napo and into the Amazon proper

A fortnight of travel brought them to Aparia the Great. Orellana and his men claimed to be the Children of the Sun and, not surprisingly, were given an especially polite welcome by their awestruck hosts. There was plenty of tasty food. This was an ideal spot, the Spaniards determined, for assembling the second brigantine. Caulked with kapok cotton and fish oil, it was launched on 24 April.

On 12 May, as the Spaniards sighted a large, bustling village, they were set upon by a large flotilla of armed canoes with warriors hidden behind tall shields and 'threatening us as if they were going to devour us'. Although two days of fierce fighting left one Spaniard dead and fifteen wounded, they managed to raid the Indians' stores of food, including several thousand turtle eggs (enough to feed 'an expeditionary force of a thousand men for a year,' adds Carvajal). The region they were now passing through – Machiparo territory – was unquestionably the most populous they had encountered so far. Then they reached Omagua land, where for more than a hundred leagues 'there was not from village to village a crossbow shot.'

Well into what is now Brazil, the party sailed past the mouth of the Japurá and into the Rió Negro.

Pizarro stated his reasons for building the first brigantine in a letter to the king. 'It was [because of] food and the problem of transporting weapons and the munitions for the harquebuses and crossbows, and of taking along the sick, and shoes for the horses, and iron bars and pickaxes and shovels and adzes, for already the greater part of the porters...had died.'

Near-contemporary views of a Napo Indian camp (opposite, above), and the Spanish party building a ship (opposite, below) and attacking an Indian village (above).

In 1587, forty-five years after Orellana's return, cartographer Joan Martines positioned Patagonia near the Río de la Plata, joined the Guyana Highlands to the Andes and combined the Orinoco and Amazon into one tremendous hydra with at least two outlets to the sea. The upper branch, apparently equivalent to the lower course of the Orinoco, is designated Río de Orellana; the lower arm extending from the Marañón is unidentified. Between the two, like a mammoth island, lay the Land of the Amazons. Yet Gaspar de Carvajal clearly stated that the women warriors who attacked them came from the north. This map inevitably brings to mind the poetic wisdom of the Incas, whose name for these huge, coiling waterways slithering into the forested periphery of their empire was *Amaru-Mayu*, 'Great Serpent-Mother of Men'.

They gave this river its name because its waters looked as black as ink. Later on the legendary rubber capital of Manaus rose at this site.

The Amazons: more than a legend?

As they went on the Spaniards put in at Indian villages, some of them fortified, and took on fresh provisions – usually at swordpoint. On 5 June 1542 they landed at a medium-sized village that Carvajal believed to be the land of the Amazons. It is a fanciful episode in his otherwise realistic account. 'In this village,' he writes, 'there was a very large public square, and in the centre was a hewn tree trunk three metres in girth, there being represented and carved in relief a walled city with its enclosure and gate. At this gate were two towers, very tall and having windows, and each tower had a door, the two facing

each other, and at each door were two columns. Two very fierce lions, which turned their glances backward, held between their forepaws and claws the entire structure, in the middle of which there was a round open space. In the centre of this space there was a hole through which they offered and poured out *chicha* for the Sun, for this is the wine which they drink. When asked by the captain what that [signified], an Indian answered that they were subjects…of the Amazons and that the only service they rendered them consisted in supplying them with feathers to line the roofs of their temples, and that the villages they had were of that kind.'

On 24 June there was a memorable encounter with 'Amazons' during a battle 'so fierce we all came very close to perishing'. 'The Amazons go about naked,' Carvajal notes, 'but with their privy parts covered, with their bows and arrows in their hands, doing as much fighting as ten Indian men.' There was another ambush the following day as they drifted close to shore, but the only casualty was Friar Carvajal. 'Our Lord saw fit that an arrow should be shot in one of my eyes, and in such a way that it went through to the other side, from which wound I have lost the eye and even now am not without suffering or free from pain.'

The Spaniards travel through a land of fantasy and hostile Indians

The expedition sailed past the mouth of the Xingu. Gradually the rain forest gave way to savanna, and the gladdened soldiers drifted across expanses of rich prairieland just waiting to be turned into wheat fields, vineyards and cattle pasture. But arrows

Depictions of Amazons from the 16th and 17th centuries. Sacred instruments (centre) are still sounded at village entrances to ward off ancestral spirits stalking the Amazonian night.

shot by 'tall men with cropped hair and skin dyed black' brought this idyll to an abrupt end. One man died in a few hours from a slight scratch; the Spaniards had just been introduced to curare.

Now fleets of several hundred canoes, each filled with twenty to forty warriors, tried to block the way as throngs cheered them on from the banks. It must have been quite a spectacle, with the reports of harquebuses punctuating drumrolls, bellowing trumpets and lilting Indian panpipes. 'They came on with a frightening din,' Carvajal reports, 'but it was a marvellous thing to see their squadrons on the riverbank dancing about and waving palm branches.'

The Arawak of the Orinoco-Negro region sent two-tone signals with slit-log drums.

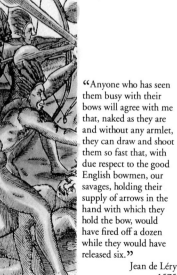

"Anyone who has seen them busy with their bows will agree with me that, naked as they are and without any armlet, they can draw and shoot them so fast that, with due respect to the good English bowmen, our savages, holding their supply of arrows in the hand with which they hold the bow, would have fired off a dozen while they would have released six."

Jean de Léry
1575

The tide was rising at a furious pace, so the Spaniards knew that the Amazon estuary could not be far off. The expedition reached Marajó Island in mid-July. Carvajal reckoned that since their departure they had covered about 7250 km. What does it matter if his calculations appear to be a little exaggerated? The important thing was that no one had ever accomplished such a journey down this river that no European, in fact, had ever known existed.

Unaware that the Portuguese settlements of Pará lay just to starboard, the explorers veered to port and into a maze of tiny islands inhabited by fearsome Carib Indians who kept them continually on the run. Then the smaller brigantine struck a stump and foundered. So it was back to making charcoal and forging iron, fighting when they weren't busy with repairs. At long last, on 26 August 1542, the banks of the river parted

"The satisfaction I have derived from watching foot soldiers with their golden [helmets] and gleaming weapons cannot compare with the pleasure I took in watching those savages fight."

Gaspar de Carvajal

The coast of Brazil, from a 1602 engraving (below).

and the sea came into view. The sailors had no charts, no compass, no sextant. They headed north and hoped for the best. The ships promptly drifted apart and each gave the other up for lost. A few days later, much to the Spaniards' surprise, both ships anchored at Cubagua, a small island off the coast of Venezuela.

Would Brazil be the site of a 'New Andalusia'?

The first journey down the Amazon had been accomplished. It had taken eight months to get from the Andes to the Atlantic. (It had taken another ten just to cross the Cordillera to the Coca.) Eleven men had perished along the way; fighting had claimed only three of them.

Gonzalo Pizarro, who had marched out of Quito with three hundred and fifty conquistadors, two hundred horses, two thousand dogs and four thousand Indians, staggered back on foot with eighty fellow Spaniards. Not one Indian, horse or dog had survived. When he arrived he learned that his brother Francisco had been assassinated in his palace and that he himself had been relieved of his duties by Emperor Charles V. No doubt out of desperation, Gonzalo raised an army and led an open revolt against the viceroy. The age of the conquistadors ended in Cuzco on 11 April 1548, when Pizarro was beheaded.

For his part, Gaspar de Carvajal went back to Lima and was later appointed archbishop. He died peacefully in 1584, at the age of eighty-two.

What became of Francisco de Orellana? His new dream was to return and colonize the lands he had just discovered, as Cortés and Francisco Pizarro had done. Off he rushed to petition the Castilian administration for the royal patent he felt was rightfully his. In 1544 he was appointed governor of the Amazon territory now officially known as the province of New Andalusia. Orellana left Spain with four ships and four hundred men, but in the New World he found that their ranks – and his dreams – crumbled before his very eyes. Twice he tried to assemble a brigantine

Although Charles V (above) happened to be born in the very year Brazil was discovered, he hardly went out of his way to continue the concern that his predecessors Ferdinand and Isabella had shown about American Indians. No doubt he was too busy implementing his new continental strategy, which, incidentally, he owed to the influx of gold from the New World. Nevertheless, the promulgation of the New Laws (1548), which prohibited Indian enslavement and recognized their status as human beings, forged a lasting link between his reign and the history of the New World. It took centuries, however, for such directives to acquire the force of law.

in the Amazon delta, as he had done before. Twice he failed, as if history refused to repeat itself.
He finally succumbed to fever and died, never again to see the main channel of the river that temporarily bore his name. For, although Francisco de Orellana was intent on calling the river he had discovered Río de las Amazonas, it was known for a while (and under protest of its namesake) as Río de Orellana – a final irony.

This engraving of Gonzalo Pizarro's execution may have been intended as an object lesson in the vagaries of chance, but the artist's staging is more reminiscent of the theatre.

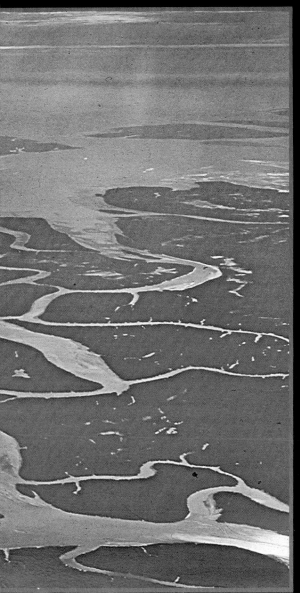

The Amazon: the great Serpent-Mother

The lower course of the Amazon looks like an inlet lazily snaking its way across a vast expanse of flat, open country. From the air the carpet of rain forest looks as unpenetrated now as it did at the dawn of time. Its monotonous basin spans 3500 km from east to west and over 1000 km from north to south. Its banks are more than 10 km apart downriver from Manaus – 1600 km in from the coast – and soon widen to about 30 km, then about 100. Extending more than 350 km from end to end, the Amazon delta envelops gigantic Marajó and the crowd of smaller islands where Caribs and Orellana fought so fiercely. Westbound ships that have not yet sighted land run into a huge plume of muddy freshwater flecked with floating jungle debris when they are still 150 km out to sea. It is the Amazon, so powerful it travels all that distance before it begins to disperse.

It is hard to tell where reality ends and imagination begins in a world that delights in blurring distinctions between life-forms – between animal, vegetable and mineral; air and water; light and shadow. A leaf can turn into a butterfly, a liana into a snake, a snake into a liana. In the 16th and 17th centuries the brooding rain forests of Amazonia witnessed an adventure-filled epic of men in pursuit of illusion.

CHAPTER 2
LIVING
LEGENDS

There are always two sides to myths and symbols – the inspirational and the sinister. Amazonia was no exception, as can be seen in this 16th-century map (left). Right, a somewhat later view of 'America'.

The legend of the Amazons does not begin with the discovery of America

Homer mentioned the Amazons as early as the 8th century BC. Through the centuries their realm, first thought to lie in the Caucasus and then in the heart of Scythia, shifted west to Cappadocia, Chaldaea, Africa, and finally to one of those mysterious islands Marco Polo had heard about. Small wonder that Christopher Columbus expected to discover this island somewhere near the New World, as did Amerigo Vespucci and other great explorers steeped in classical culture.

Indeed, the Isle of the Amazons shifted so far west that one day it emerged from the ocean and ended up deep in the tropical rain forest we now call Amazonia.

But Friar Carvajal's account infused the myth with a freshness and plausibility it had never had before. In 1542, for the first time ever, the fierce women warriors had actually been seen, even engaged in combat. The people who took part in the adventure said so themselves.

Even though the Spanish court did not take Orellana's reports

"Conquered and seized by the Greeks, we read in Herodotus, the Amazons fled to the land of the free-ranging Scythians. 'We would have you for our wives,' they said, to which the women replied, 'Nay.... Your women abide in their wagons working at women's crafts and never go abroad a-hunting or for aught else.'"

seriously, a symbolic chain reaction rooted deep in our collective unconscious had been triggered in the imaginations of everyone intrigued by the mystery of equatorial America. It swept history along with it and took several centuries to subside.

Various views of the Amazons in relief, tapestry and engraving.

The myths of the Amazons and El Dorado soon become inseparable

At that time the Cordillera of the Andes was believed to be the home of an overlord known as El Dorado. According to tradition he would be coated with gold dust and ritually immersed in what has since been identified as Lake Guatavita (near Bogotá) while sacrificial offerings of jewels and vessels were thrown into the water.

The truth of the matter was that his powerful altiplano neighbours, the Chibcha, had dethroned him even before the Spanish arrived on the scene. But what did history matter? Turning their backs on the Andes, the Spaniards sought El Dorado – and the Amazons – far from there, northeast of the Río Negro, at a place on the western edge of the Guiana Highlands where cartographers drew a fabulous lake bigger than the Caspian Sea. In time, once imagination gave way to geographical fact, Lake Parima became Sierra Parima, mountainous source of the Orinoco.

"We draw the bow, throw the javelin, ride horses. We are not housewives!"
Jacques Lacarrière

The shores of this mythical lake were thought to be the site of a city of stone 'that far exceeds any of the world, at least so much of it as is known to the Spanish nation'. This was the capital city of Manoa, supposed home of El Dorado, now described as a 'great emperor'. A man named Juan Martínez had reportedly lived there for seven months.

'He was not allowed to wander into the country anywhere. He was also brought thither all the way blindfolded....After Martínez had lived seven months in Manoa and began to understand the language of the country, Inga [the emperor] asked him whether he desired to return to his own country or would willingly abide with him. But Martínez, not desirous to stay, obtained the favour of Inga to depart, with whom he sent divers Guianians to conduct him to the River Orinoco, all laden with as much gold as they could carry, which he gave to

El Dorado (below left) was said to live in Manoa, whose size befitted a legendary city. According to Sir Walter Raleigh, Juan Martínez reportedly walked its streets for more than a day before reaching the emperor's palace.

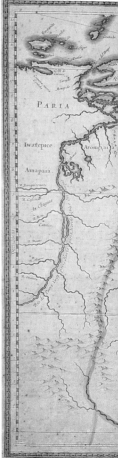

Martínez at his departure. But when he arrived near the river's side, the borderers, which are called Orinocoponi, robbed him and his Guianians of all the treasure…save only two great gourd bottles filled with beads of gold curiously wrought, which those Orinocoponi thought was [his] drink…. So in canoes he fell down by the river of Orinoco to Trinidad, and from thence to Puerto Rico…. For the abundance of

So vast it's a wonder that no one ever saw it, Lake Parima (here in a Dutch map of 1630) was by far the biggest and most persistent hoax ever perpetrated by geographers. It took two centuries for them to remove it from their maps.

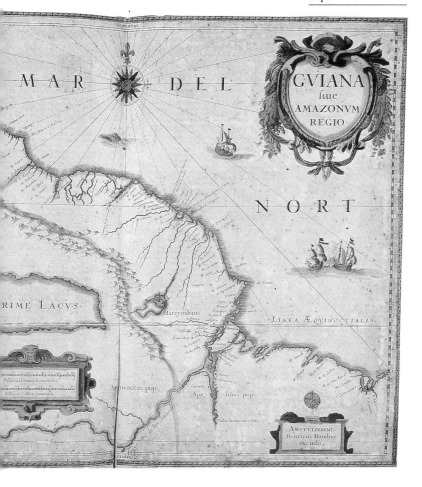

gold which he saw in the city, the images of gold in their temples, the plates, armours and shields of gold which they use in their wars, he called the city El Dorado.' At any rate, that is what Sir Walter Raleigh, favourite of Queen Elizabeth I, claimed to have read in the papers of the governor of Trinidad, whom he had taken prisoner.

The realm of the Amazons was believed to lie near Manoa. According to Martínez, 'these women...wear long dresses of fine wool and golden crowns several inches across. They accompany with men but once in a year. If they conceive and be delivered of a son, they return him to the father, if of a daughter, they nourish it and retain it. All being desirous to increase their own sex and kind, as many as have daughters send unto the begetters a present...a kind of green stone known only to them.'

After languishing in the Tower of London for thirteen years Sir Walter Raleigh (above) made a second voyage to the fabulous land of El Dorado in search of the greatest adventure of them all. He then returned to England – and the block.

Sir Walter Raleigh forsakes the pomp of the English court and sets sail in search of Manoa

Nobleman, occasional poet, privateer if not pirate, Raleigh was a larger-than-life figure who never abandoned his dreams. Raleigh weaves into his account, *The Discovery of the Empire of Guiana*, particulars about the two myths that compelled him to leave everything behind. His description of the land of the Amazons enlarges on and further embellishes Carvajal's: 'Their cities, all built of stone, are connected by paved roads, these being lined with walls, which have at their entrance manned gates opened only to those who pay a toll. Round about, herds of vicuña graze in rich pastures.'

Like miniatures in an equatorial Book of Hours, Raleigh's tableaux present the future Green Hell as an earthly paradise. 'I never saw a more beautiful country, nor more likely prospects, hills so raised here and there over the valleys, the river winding into diverse branches, the plains adjoining without bush or stubble, all fair green grass, the ground of hard sand easy to march on, either for horse or foot, the deer crossing in every path, the birds toward the evening singing on every tree with a thousand several tunes, cranes and herons of white, crimson and carnation perching on the riverside. The air fresh with a gentle easterly wind, and every stone we stooped to take up, promised either gold or silver by its complexion.

Seen welcoming Indians in the 16th-century engraving below, Raleigh began writing his monumental (and, sadly, unfinished) *History of the World* while in the Tower of London.

Your Majesty shall see of many sorts, and I hope some of them cannot be bettered under the sun.' The region had so many of these stones, all one had to do was bend down and pick them up. 'The Spaniards call it "The Mother of Gold",' adds Raleigh without further comment.

Unfortunately, Queen Elizabeth died soon afterwards. Raleigh's second voyage ended with a retreat to the Antilles. For all his fertile imagination, this adventurer and reputed Prince Charming did not prove as fortunate as Scheherazade and, like Gonzalo Pizarro, was beheaded on his return to London in 1618.

The wonders of the past go hand in hand with the exploration of the New World

Christopher Columbus had set the tone in a ship's log that sometimes reads like the adventures of Sinbad. He fully expected to find Cyclopes ('men

The Ewaipanoma (also called Acephali, 'headless men') may have been the present-day Yekuana, a Carib people of northern Venezuela.

with a single eye in the middle of the forehead') on the island of Cuba and felt sure that equally strange creatures 'with snouts of dogs, who ate men' lay in wait nearby.

But Amazonia, it seemed, sheltered even greater wonders. After describing the Tivitiva, who 'dwell upon the trees', Raleigh writes about the Acephali, deformed creatures famous throughout Europe for their monstrous anatomy.

Perhaps these were Pliny's Blemmi, then thought to dwell in Africa. If so, their reappearance was short-lived. Captain Laurence Keymis, who took part in Raleigh's second voyage (1617), made the following entry in his diary: 'A cacique [local chieftain] imparted to me particulars relative to the headless men, said to have their mouths in the middle of their breasts. The legend of the Acephali originated from the fact that these people are given to keeping their shoulders in a raised position,

Everything about this land was alien and defied conventional logic. As these 16th-century engravings demonstrate, the first Europeans to set foot in Amazonia let their imaginations run away with them and claimed actually to see and hear everything they had hitherto only imagined: from the works of Pliny to Herodotus, from the words of Arabian storytellers to Mogul writers, from tales of knightly derring-do to medieval hagiographies, from cathedral gargoyles to the all-too-lifelike visions of Hieronymus Bosch. Seldom have reality and fantasy complemented each other so well.

The fanatical missionaries who started hounding the 'savages' of Amazonia in the 16th century were largely responsible for the exodus of Indian populations towards the interior. Forced to defend themselves against a systematic assault on customs and beliefs dismissed out of hand as devil worship, the Indians unreluctantly slaughtered their overzealous intruders when they saw fit. The missionaries (including the Spanish priest Ferrer in 1611, left, and another, anonymous, missionary, opposite), in turn, saw the chance to earn the crown of martyrdom as a further incentive and redoubled their efforts. This conflict did not begin to subside until Christendom acknowledged the right of every individual to be different.

as they consider this deformity graceful.'

By then, the tug-of-war between history and legend, fact and fiction, was already well under way. In 1575 André Thevet, a Frenchman who had spent three months in Brazil, retracted what he had said about the Amazons in *Les Singularités de la France antarctique* (*Peculiarities of Equatorial France*): 'They are not Amazons, only unfortunate women who endeavour to preserve their lives, children and property while their husbands are away.'

In 1560 Lope de Aguirre, an obscure subordinate officer, proclaims himself king of Amazonia

Was there anything to the stories about El Dorado, Lake Parima and the fabulous city of Manoa? To answer this question, in 1560, less than twenty years after Orellana's expedition, the viceroy of Peru instructed a Spanish general, Pedro de Ursúa, to journey across the Cordillera and find out for himself.

No sooner had Ursúa's hastily raised band of men reached the Amazon than a Basque named Lope de Aguirre mutinied, executed his general and proclaimed himself not only commander of the detachment but king of Amazonia. And anyone unwilling to follow him would be thrown to the crocodiles!

As Aguirre headed north in search of the Guiana Highlands, did he unknowingly discover the Casiquiare, a natural waterway linking the Orinoco and the Negro rivers, more than a century before Humboldt did? Be that as it may, he emerged at the mouth of the Orinoco, across from Trinidad; and after seizing Margarita, the island of the pearl fishers, he was defeated by royalist troops from Venezuela and, needless to say, sentenced to death.

Before he was beheaded, he reportedly uttered the following brief prayer, probably the only one ever to pass his lips: 'Lord, if you intend to do me a good turn, do so right away. Save your glory for your saints.' A fitting epilogue to his story.

Gonzalo Pizarro, Lope de Aguirre, Sir Walter Raleigh – heroes or cutthroats, they all lost their heads over Amazonia in more ways than one. Aside from rapacity, the only thing these men had in common was their craving for the superhuman and the wondrous.

At the end of his long odyssey, Lope de Aguirre ruled supreme over Margarita Island for two months after killing the governor and leading officials. Bent on carving out a bigger empire for himself in Venezuela, he then decided to head back to the mainland, where, forsaken by his men (and, the story goes, weary of being a professional cutthroat), he fell into the hands of Spanish royalists and was executed.

Missionaries in the Amazonian rain forest

Fresh attempts were made to penetrate Amazonia early in the 17th century. Even before reaching the

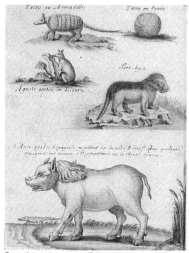

main river channel, several missionaries lost their lives at the hands of the same Indians who had clashed so fiercely with Gonzalo Pizarro.

Still, the missionaries' time had come. Following in the footsteps of the conquistadors, Jesuit priests and Dominican friars established numerous, if temporary, missions and in so doing became the first to compile valuable ethnographic and linguistic information. On one occasion, Jesuit priest Cristobal de Acuña reports, a canoe with two missionaries and six Spanish soldiers drifted downstream to Pará, near the mouth of the Amazon, 'and all they could tell us was that they had come from Peru, seen many Indians, and dared not go back the way they had come.'

A Portuguese captain, Pedro de Teixeira, is the first to journey from Pará to Quito – and back

One day, nearly a century after Orellana's discovery jolted the world – especially the rival courts of the Iberian peninsula – the governor of Pará, who resided in the new city of Belém, finally decided to organize an expedition. He instructed a veteran, Captain Teixeira, to journey up to Quito and record

The armadillo, as described by Sir Walter Raleigh: 'A beast called by the Spaniards *Armadilla*...seemeth to be barred over with small plates somewhat like to a *Renocero*, with a white horne growing in its hinder parts, as big as a great hunting horne, which they use to winde instead of a trumpet. Monardus [a physician] writeth that a little of the powder of that horn put into the eare, cureth deafnes.'

Sixteenth-century explorer Jean de Léry accurately describes the agouti as 'a reddish-brown creature the size of a month-old pig, which has cloven hooves, a very short tail, ears much like those of a hare, and very good to eat.'

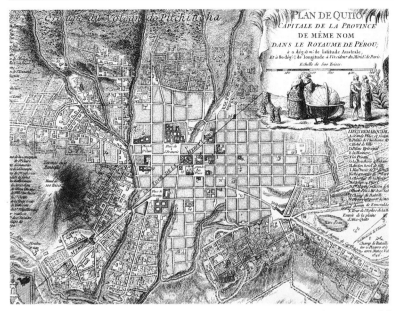

everything he deemed noteworthy along the way.

Teixeira crossed the Pará border on 28 October 1637 with a flotilla of forty-six canoes laden with sixty Portuguese soldiers, twelve hundred Indians and sundry wives and guides – some two thousand people in all. Before it was over, more than half of them were to run away.

Even so, the first journey up the Amazon was completed in the record time of eight months. On 24 June 1638 Teixeira reached the first Spanish settlement, near Quito.

The Amazons, according to a Dominican friar and a Jesuit priest

The astute viceroy of Peru gave the Portuguese a polite welcome and promptly directed that Teixeira be provided with whatever equipment he would need for the trip back, including, as Father Acuña notes, the assistance of 'two individuals in whom the crown of

What conqueror did not eventually turn into a builder of cities? The Spanish were no exception. No sooner had Pizarro seized the Inca empire than he started planning its facelift. Atahualpa was put to death in 1533; his dynasty expired with him. In 1534 Sebastián de Benalcázar, Pizarro's lieutenant, razed the capital city and mapped out a new Quito with a Spanish-style grid of streets. Set like a jewel amid mountain peaks, this priceless vestige of Jesuit architecture 2800 metres above sea level has been remarkably well preserved.

Castile can place its trust regarding everything that
has been discovered thus far and which is likely to be
during this return voyage.'

The *corregidor* of Quito himself personally
volunteered for the mission; instead, Crown officials
chose Acuña, who had recently arrived from Spain to
found a Jesuit college.

Thus, a hundred years separate the first two
accounts of the discovery of the River of the Amazons
– one by a Dominican, the other by a Jesuit. In
December 1639 Acuña reached Belém and
immediately set sail for Spain, as he had been
instructed to do. His book, *The New Discovery of the
Great Amazon River*, was published in 1641.
Comparisons between Acuña's and Carvajal's
narratives are as interesting as they are inevitable.

Before proceeding to the journey itself, Acuña
pointedly states that some accounts
'may not always be as truthful as they
ought to be' – a passing gibe at
Carvajal. 'But this one will be, and
indeed I shall allege nothing I myself
cannot attest to with my head held
high, and more than fifty Spaniards,
Castilians and Portuguese who made
the same trip will vouch for those
things declared as certain or dubious,
as the case may be.'

Yet, from the very first chapter, he
makes a case for the Amazons,
arguing that he heard about them
wherever he went and that 'the
details, on which there is universal
agreement, are so precise, it is
impossible that a fiction should have
entered into so many languages and
be met with among so many natives.'

Certain details of Father Acuña's
description of the Amazons bear
repeating, if only to show his

The classicism of these
all'antica figures is
more like a drawing by
Michelangelo than the
sketchbook of an explorer
in the New World. These
illustrations from Jean de
Léry's account of his
voyage to Brazil (1555-8)
depict scenes from the
life of the famous man-eating
Tupinambá.

tendency to wax lyrical. 'As a rule, these worthy women have no commerce with men. Even when those [men] with whom they do have intercourse make their annual visit, they do not welcome them without weapons in hand – bows and arrows – and so remain until such time as they have judged the men and are satisfied that they have indeed come in peace; whereupon they lay down their arms and run to their guests' canoes. Each of them takes hold of a suitable hammock – which is what the men sleep in – and carries it back to her hut and hangs it up heaven knows where.'

His conclusion, however, is equivocal. 'Time will reveal the truth about this, and whether these are indeed the famous Amazons, and if their land holds treasures which might enrich the whole world.'

"It was wonderful to hear the women, who yelled so loudly it sounded like the howling of dogs and wolves. 'He is dead!' some of them wailed, 'he who was so brave and gave us so many prisoners to eat.' Whereupon the others replied, 'What a good hunter and excellent fisherman he was!' Then one of them cried out, 'Oh, our avenger, our gallant slaughterer of Portuguese!'"

Jean de Léry

Tableau des principaux P

We need look no further than this classicizing, indeed courtly, tableau of prettified Indians by a contemporary of Jean-Jacques Rousseau to see that the age of the 'noble savage' had arrived. Paradoxically, even as rapid strides were being made in objective documentation of the new continent, the way its inhabitants were being portrayed was never farther from the truth.

Particulars about Indian life and customs in Acuña's account

Certain aspects of Acuña's narrative signal the approach of the Enlightenment, and from them we can gauge the progress that had been made in the century between his account and Carvajal's. He documented not only animal and plant species indigenous to the Amazon and its banks, but plants the Indians cultivated, the tools they used, their customs, their hunting and fishing techniques. Even if these notations fall short of bona fide scientific observations, at least they provide evidence for an emerging shift away from fantasy.

Acuña points out that the Amazon's four principal resources are wood, cocoa (which in those days grew wild along the riverbank), tobacco and sugarcane, followed by cotton, sarsaparilla, gums, resins and pharmaceutical oils. Add mineral deposits, and you have a complete rundown of what was to become – and still is – the backbone of Amazonia's economy.

Yet, a few pages later, this conscientious observer reports the existence of giants 'ten to sixteen spans' (over three metres) tall; of dwarfs 'no bigger than tender babies', known as the Guyazi; and of 'people with their feet turned backward, so that pursuers track them in the wrong direction'.

By the end of the 17th century Amazonia has been incorporated into the Brazilian empire

Acuña concludes that the banks of the Amazon, 'paragon of rivers', are 'paradises of fertility, and if art abetted the richness of the soil, there would be nothing but peaceful gardens along its entire length'. Acuña's discourse reeks of the courtier. 'Though it holds magnificent riches, it is open to all. Indeed, it magnanimously bids people from every walk of life

An American native, the tobacco plant.

to profit therefrom: to the poor, it offers sustenance; to the labourer, his fill of work; to the tradesman, business; to the soldier, the road to glory; to the rich, newfound wealth; to the powerful, lands to govern; and to the king himself, a whole new empire.'

This undisguised invitation notwithstanding, Spain did not attempt to wrest Amazonia from Portugal. The six million square kilometres that comprise the bulk of the basin were to remain a permanent part of Brazil. But this vast plain was to be ringed by a Castilian Amazonia bordered by present-day Venezuela, Colombia, Ecuador, Peru and Bolivia.

By the end of the 17th century the partition of Amazonia was complete; Spain and Portugal had been the only real contenders. English, French and Dutch navigators found their claims shunted to the north, to the other side of the Guiana Highlands.

For all intents and purposes, the establishment of a fort at Belém on 20 January 1616 signalled the beginning of Portugal's annexation of Amazonia. Once the other Europeans withdrew and Captain Teixeira completed his journey to Quito, the next stage of Portuguese penetration was the fort at Barra (1669) – the future Manaus. Magistrates along the river soon outnumbered even soldiers.

"With an enthusiasm that bridged every barrier, they climbed the Andes, they swept down dark mysterious rivers, they trekked across the deserts and struggled through the Laocoön entanglements of its firefly-spangled jungles.… America [was] investigated, codified and put into a literature that freed the continent completely from the fantasies which had flourished for three hundred years."

Victor Wolfgang von Hagen
South America Called Them

CHAPTER 3

THE AGE OF REASON PENETRATES THE RAIN FOREST

Fauna, flora and crafts of Amazonia from 19th-century lithographs.

Just as exactly one century (1540 to 1640) separated the first two books about the exploration of the Amazon, a hundred years elapsed between Acuña's chronicle and what could be called the first scientific account of a journey down the Amazon.

La Condamine: Amazonia's window on modern times

In 1745 the French Academy of Sciences in Paris heard Charles Marie de La Condamine read his *Abridged Narrative of Travels Through the Interior of South America, From the Shores of the Pacific Ocean to the Coasts of Brazil and Guiana, Descending the River of the Amazons.*

The stated purpose of La Condamine's expedition was to settle a purely scientific controversy: did the earth bulge at the equator and flatten out at the poles, as Newton maintained, or vice versa? A team of botanists, astronomers and the most distinguished savants of the 18th century set out with La Condamine on a journey to Quito to calculate the exact length of a degree of longitude when measured at the equator. Once his official mission had been accomplished, La Condamine decided to stay and embark on a journey down the Amazon. His account does not so much separate fact from fiction as cross-fade them (to borrow a term from cinematography), blurring myth at the same time as bringing objective description into sharper focus.

INTRODUCTI
HISTORIQUE
ou
JOURNAL DES TRAV
DES ACADEMICIEN
Envoyés par ordre du Roi sous l'Eq
Depuis 1735 jusqu'en 1745.

Tous ceux qui ont pris quelque part à la q la Figure de la Terre, ont remarqué avec surp ans ont à peine suffi pour terminer notre voyage. O estimé la durée à quatre tout au plus : encore sup alors, conformément au premier projet, qu'outre du méridien, à laquelle nos opérations se sont born rapporterions celle de quelques degrés de l'équateu de travail dont les ordres du Roi nous ont depuis di

D'ailleurs on sait que le voyage au cercle pol le plan ne fut formé qu'après notre départ, & que d'un degré, dans les régions incultes & souvent

A

Charles Marie de La Condamine (left) on curare: 'It will no doubt occasion surprise that among a people who possess an instrument so certain and so quick of effect with which to satiate their vengeance, jealousy or hate, it should be fatal to monkeys and birds alone. It is the more to be admired that a missionary, ever dreaded and often held in abhorrence by his neophytes,...should live without fear or mistrust of harm.'

"Though no remaining vestige should be found of this feminine republic, this would not yet prove that none such had ever existed.... If ever such a nation [of Amazons] did exist, it must have been in America, where the frequent wanderings of the women, who often accompany their husbands to war, and the hardships of their domestic life might originate [the] idea of shaking off the yoke of their tyrants."
La Condamine

La Condamine focuses on the question of the Amazons

First, he noted a consistency of detail in the folklores of peoples otherwise so mutually alien as to rule out any suspicion of complicity. Everything, he wrote, led him to believe that after migrating from south to north, the women warriors settled in the heart of Guiana. Later, in 1800, Alexander von Humboldt assumed 'not that there are Amazons...but that

Gorges along the Amazon, 1745 engraving.

women in different parts of America, wearied of the state of slavery in which they were held by men, united themselves together, like the fugitive Negroes.'

That fastidious intellectuals like La Condamine and Humboldt did not debunk the myth directly may come as a surprise. Since stories about the Amazons were so widespread and persistent, they probably did not feel they had enough hard evidence to settle the issue of 'feminine republics in the New World'. We should point out, however, that at about this time a few informed observers with firsthand knowledge of the Indian world seemed more than willing to deflate the legend. The captain of the frigate *Solano*, dispatched by the king of Spain to oversee the first official demarcation of Portuguese Brazil from Spanish Venezuela, mentions in 1756 that Guipuinavi women, particularly newlyweds, fought alongside their husbands and displayed exceptional bravery – understandably so, he adds, as they were hot-tempered and were taught, like boys, how to handle a bow and shield from early childhood. 'These women or others like them', he concludes, 'must be the Amazons Orellana saw fighting among the men, because, then as now, women from here [the upper Orinoco] to the Amazon joined in the fighting.'

Accurate information about mountains and rivers is gradually incorporated into maps

Without Amazons, the imagination was losing ground in Amazonia. The women warriors were the first to go. Then Lake Parima, the fabulous city of

"Alexander von Humboldt [left] has been with me for some hours this morning. What an extraordinary man he is! Though I have known him so long, I am always newly amazed by him. He possesses a versatility of genius which I have never seen equalled. Whatever may be the subject broached, he seems quite at home with it, and showers upon us treasures in profusion from his stores of knowledge. He is like a fountain with many spouts; one need only proffer vessels to collect its precious and inexhaustible flow."

Goethe

Humboldt crossing the Cordillera (right), from a 19th-century engraving.

Manoa and the palace of El Dorado disappeared from the map. Commissions with geometers and surveyors started to demarcate boundaries across what was still largely unexplored terrain.

One long-standing error, attributable in large part to the El Dorado legend, involved the location of the Guiana Highlands. Another perpetuated the difficulty in distinguishing between the Orinoco and Amazon river systems.

In the late 18th century people finally realized that the river Colombians upstream called the Putumayo and Brazilians downstream called the Içá were, in fact, the same major tributary flowing down from the Andean Cordillera into the Amazon, and that likewise the Japurá and Caquetá were simply Brazilian and Colombian names, respectively, for the same waterway. Neither of these two rivers flowed directly into the Orinoco or the Negro, as had long been thought. Farther north, the Meta, Vichada and Guaviare, which run more or less parallel to

La Condamine had already raised the question of possible links between the Amazon and Orinoco basins. To settle it, Humboldt journeyed up the Orinoco in 1800, travelling, as locals did, in *falcas*, large, half-decked canoes with palm-branch roofs. Motorized versions of the same kind of craft ply the Negro and upper Orinoco to this day.

the Içá and the Japurá, turned out to be branches of the Orinoco.

The Casiquiare River, the connection between the Negro and Orinoco.

Humboldt is credited with discovering the link between the Orinoco and the Amazon

The question was not whether a link between these two mighty rivers existed – there were too many accounts of it to doubt that – but how they were connected and where. After all, if there was no link, how could Indian flotillas encountered in one river turn up in the other? How could Lope de Aguirre have left the Amazon and reached the sea by way of the Orinoco delta? In 1742 a woman claiming to be from Venezuela had made her way to Brazil by way of what she said was a river flowing from the Orinoco to the Río Negro. Two years later some Jesuits reported that a missionary from the Negro sailed upstream to call on the superior of the Orinoco missions; the two of them sailed back down together by the same route.

The earliest authoritative maps of the region were

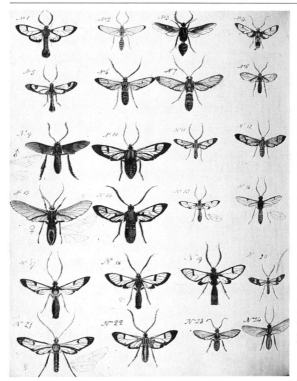

The Industrial Revolution of mid-19th-century England left in its wake a new breed of scientific researcher, one that did not depend on privilege to make good. Consider Henry Walter Bates and Alfred Russel Wallace, still remembered for their contributions to natural science. When they first met and found that they shared a dream of adventure, one was a surveyor's assistant, the other a hosier's apprentice. The British Museum commissioned them to compile a collection of insects and plants – at threepence for every specimen received 'in saleable condition' – and in 1848 they landed at Belém with nothing to declare but their enthusiasm.

A fish Wallace discovered during his travels on the Negro.

riddled with inaccuracies. Sanson based his on the observations of Father Acuña. The second map (1707), which reflected forty-five years of fieldwork by Father Samuel Fritz, a German Jesuit, was already closer to the mark. It took another hundred years to see the light. But in this land of disproportion, where so much water flows simultaneously in so many different directions, how could the matter have been puzzled out any sooner?

Alexander von Humboldt's achievement was to describe in black and white the course of the

Casiquiare River, which he himself had negotiated in 1800 from its confluence with the Negro to its starting point on the upper Orinoco. Once and for all, the Andes and Guiana Highlands were correctly assigned their respective waterways.

That the Casiquiare really existed and was navigable was truly momentous news, coming as it did on the eve of an Industrial Revolution that was to change the face of the world and expand trade between the continents on either side of the Atlantic.

River dwellers began to move away in droves. La Condamine was the first to call attention to the irreversible exodus the arrival of soldiers and missionaries had precipitated. 'More than a century ago,' he writes, 'the banks…were peopled with a great variety of nations, who withdrew to the interior at the sight of the Europeans.'

'These devoted, hard-working men plying the Amazon have come not to ravage, but to study'

That was how the botanist, zoologist and early ethnographer Alcide d'Orbigny characterized the scientist-scholars of the 19th century. The era of great scientific explorers did, in fact, coincide with a relative lull in the slaughtering of Indians. Although the

Henry Walter Bates spent eleven years in Amazonia and brought back 14,712 specimens, including eight thousand species unknown to science. He became a luminary in the field of entomology and advanced the theory of mimicry, which helped pave the way for the discovery of the evolution of species. Two of his drawings are shown above and left.

Alfred Russel Wallace, the father of zoogeography, spent four years on the Río Negro. A precursor of the theory of evolution, he sent Darwin his paper on natural selection, which was read to the Linnaean Society in London at the same time as the first draft of the renowned *Origin of Species*.

majority of them were naturalists –
botanists for the most part – they were
all 'philosophers' in the tradition of the
Enlightenment and, like Humboldt,
generalists. (In those happy times
specialization did not preclude working
in several fields at once.) They
spontaneously pioneered Amazonian
ethnography. Their accounts are our
window on the lives of what were at the
time still undisturbed Indian groups.
The fact that most of these peoples are
now totally acculturated, when they
have survived at all, makes the work all
the more intriguing.

Long, frequent journeys were now the
rule as many Europeans crossed the
ocean. Botanist Auguste de
Saint-Hilaire trekked across thousands

"They wrap a rope
around its neck, suspend
it from a tree and
clamber up the snake like
a mast until they reach
the neck, then slit its
throat with a knife and
ease themselves down to
the ground, cutting it
open along the entire
length of its body."

Malte-Brun

of miles of Brazilian jungle to compile an herbarium.
D'Orbigny ranged across the continent and returned
to Paris with a collection of 100,000 valuable
specimens that form the basis of numerous studies to
this day. There was also the team of Johann Baptist
von Spix and Karl Friedrich Philipp von Martius –
and many others from many other countries.

The popularity these scientists enjoyed was fuelled
by the enthusiasm of a century that clamoured for
fresh discoveries. Public opinion in Europe spurred
them to action and helped to release the funds they
needed for their undertakings. The magazine *Le Tour
du Monde* thought nothing of publishing Paul
Marcoy's account of his fourteen-year odyssey from
the deserts of coastal Peru to Belém – for three years
running! Not since the chronicles of the Spanish
Conquest had so much been added to our under-
standing of the continent. The mounds of notes,
collections and specimens they brought back with
them have been an inexhaustible resource for
scientists and historians ever since.

A giant water lily big enough for a coiled boa to snooze on

The countless discoveries made in Amazonia at this time range from the amusing to the deadly serious, from the picturesque to the momentous. In the 1840s, while exploring what was then British Guiana, the botanist Robert Schomburgk stumbled across a spectacular water lily of gigantic proportions. Stretching about two metres across, the pad looked like an enormous dinner plate and could have easily supported a coiled boa dozing in the shade of its tremendous blossom, which boasted an expansive corolla that ran the gamut of pink between its pearly white petals and bright red centre. Here was a flower worthy of Amazonian excess. The chivalrous Schomburgk christened the future pride of botanical gardens *Victoria regia* in honour of the British sovereign. But there were even more valuable, if less benign, discoveries to come, discoveries that once again turned the River of the Amazons into the stuff that myths are made of.

Henry Bates catching a crocodile, one of the two most spectacular monsters of Amazonian waters. The black caiman can reach five to six metres in length; its cousin along the Caribbean coast, *Crocodylus intermedius*, can reportedly exceed eight metres. Some people claim that anacondas (opposite) can grow to twelve metres and weigh more than 150 kilos.

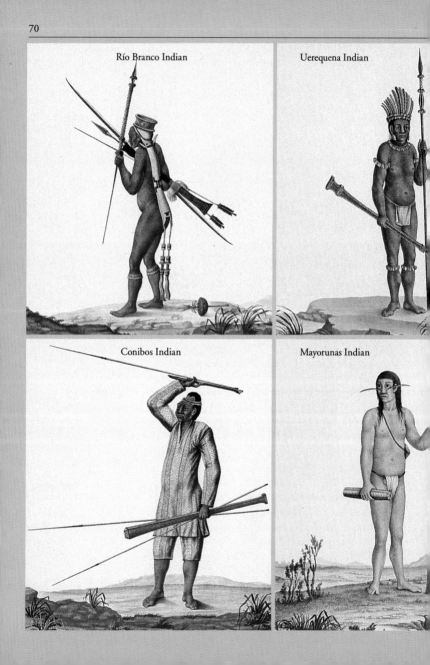

Río Branco Indian

Uerequena Indian

Conibos Indian

Mayorunas Indian

Uaupé Indian

Macuxy Indian

Philosophical journey

Between 1783 and 1792 a group of Portuguese explorer-scholars gained prominence by compiling the century's most valuable collection of illustrations devoted to Amazonian Indians and fauna. Alexandre Rodrigues Ferreira was a doctor of 'natural philosophy' at the University of Coimbra; his travelling companions, Joaquim José Codina and José Joaquim Freire, were artists from the Royal Natural History Collection in Lisbon. They painted continuously for nine years while ranging about 40,000 km (a distance equivalent to the circumference of the earth) along the Negro, Branco, Madeira, Guaporé and Mamoré rivers. Surprises awaited them at every turn; they were the first, if not to see, at least to record them with photographic precision. One such discovery, a device used to propel arrows or javelins, is one of humanity's oldest weapons, predating even the bow (opposite, lower left).

Hummingbird

Trogon

Porcupine

Black
Spider
Monkey

Howler Monkey

Peccary

Collared Anteater

Woolly Spider Monkey

The science of illustration

Testimony to their unerring powers of observation, Codina's and Freire's illustrations for the *Diario da Viagem Fillosofica* (*Journal of a Philosophical Voyage*) lavish as much detail on indigenous Amazonian wildlife as they do on Indian weaponry and adornment. Known to Brazilians as the *beija-flor*, or 'kiss-flower', the tiny, brightly coloured hummingbird looks like a masterpiece of precious enamelwork. The peccary, a local food staple because of its tasty, nourishing meat, lives in herds of up to a hundred individuals. The Indians hunt them with spears, but are careful not to squander nature's bounty and take only what they intend to eat or cure for the rainy season, which is their winter. The spider monkey is the only one in the world that swings from branch to branch using its arms and prehensile tail. The name of the bulkier, more sedentary howler monkey is misleading, for the sound it makes in the forest at sunrise and nightfall is closer to a moan than a howl.

Cotinga

Piranha

Snowy Egret

Cock-of-the-Rock

Matamata

Morocoy, or Jabuti

Crocodile

The misadventures of a manuscript

The reputation of the piranha (or cannibal-fish, from *caribe*, its name along the Orinoco) is well established. It should be noted, however, that it is not tiny, as was once thought, but as big as a carp. The cock-of-the-rock is coveted by collectors of American birds everywhere for its elegant saffron plumage and fan-shaped crest. Lastly, the matamata, a bizarre turtle that looks as though its head was caught in a funnel, has a distinctive non-retractile neck and must swing its head in under its carapace sideways. Ferreira's monumental collection reached Lisbon unscathed, only to face fresh perils. Geoffroy Saint-Hilaire made off with it during the Napoleonic Conquest, and Ferreira died in 1815 resigned to the permanent loss of his life's work. The manuscripts were recovered but subsequently dispersed and not recompiled for another century.

"A tree called *heve* grows in the province of Esmeraldas. With a single incision it secretes a milky-white fluid that gradually hardens and darkens on contact with air.... The Mayan Indians call the resin obtained therefrom *cauchu*, which is pronounced *cahouchou* and means 'tree-that-weeps'."

Charles Marie de La Condamine

CHAPTER 4

THE GREAT RUBBER ADVENTURE

In the 19th century the rain forest was invaded by rubber-hungry businessmen.

This comment about the rubber tree was of particular interest to the learned assembly that convened at the French Academy of Sciences in Paris to hear La Condamine read his *Abridged Narrative*.

'From the Omaguas the Portuguese of Pará learned the method of forming syringes of the same matter, and pumps which need no sucker. These syringes are made in the shape of a pear, with a neck at the extremity, that, as well as the body, being hollow. Into this neck a cane is fitted.... This, when full being suddenly pressed, the contained fluid is expelled with the same effect as from a syringe. Among the Omaguas it is a very common utensil. When they assemble on occasion of an entertainment, the master of the house never fails to present one of these bottles to each of his guests, and its contents are voided constantly previous to the beginning of a grand dinner.'

Thus, one of the greatest conquests in the history of modern industrial technology can be traced back to Amazonian syringes and nozzles. Brazilians recall it every time they refer to a stand of wild rubber trees as a *seringue* or a rubber tapper as a *seringueiro*.

La Condamine's remarks about the Omagua call for further comment. They filled their syringes with a narcotic substance that could be inhaled or administered as an enema, and the use of drugs accounts for their sharing of the device at gatherings. The first rubber object made in Europe, the pencil rubber, was invented by English chemist Joseph Priestley. He called it 'India-rubber'.

Indians have long made expert use of rubber

Amazonian peoples have long been expert users of wild rubber. In the 19th century the Omagua Indians demonstrated the use of a rubber syringe to the Portuguese.

The ball the Maya of Mesoamerica played with was made of rubber, as it was wherever this game is known to have existed (the Taino of Haiti, the Apinayé of central Brazil). The Indians along the upper Orinoco coated drumsticks with rubber. Damp wood caught fire more easily when some of the gum was added to it, and it proved handy for caulking leaks in canoes. As far back as the early 18th century the Indians showed the Portuguese of Pará how latex could be moulded into boots and containers, or used as a waterproof coating for canvas.

Macintosh, Hancock, Goodyear, Michelin, Dunlop – names that have become symbols

Although the growing popularity of bicycles and cars was largely responsible for the tremendous surge in world demand that began in 1850 and triggered the great Amazonian rubber rush, credit must also go to a handful of inventors and their now-legendary discoveries. In 1823 a Scotsman named Charles Macintosh won instant fame for manufacturing rubber-coated fabric. Seven years later Thomas Hancock perfected a process to make raw rubber pliable. In 1839 Charles Goodyear discovered vulcanization, which paved the way for the production of the first pneumatic tyre.

From then on the history of rubber and the car went hand in hand. In 1888 while tinkering with his ten-year-old son's tricycle, an Irish veterinary surgeon named John Boyd Dunlop invented the first pneumatic rubber tyre, which he eventually patented. Four years later Edouard Michelin made the first detachable pneumatic rubber tyre.

The boom was on. Demand for rubber skyrocketed. With a monopoly on wild rubber trees and the freedom to set its own prices, Amazonia became a vast equatorial Klondike. The precious commodity flowed down the Marañón, Ucayali, Javari, Madeira, Napo, Putumayo, Caquetá and Negro rivers from Bolivia, Peru, Ecuador and Colombia, converging on Manaus. As the closest deepwater port offering year-round access to ocean-going ships, the city emerged as the rubber capital of the world. With its unique floating docks loaded with rubber, soon Manaus was awash in gold and poised for an era of unbridled luxury. Were the stories that spurred the Conquest about to come true after all?

Mythical Manoa gives way to the living legend of Manaus

In the early 19th century what is now Manaus was Barra, a garrison village that grew from a small fort the Portuguese had built in 1669 to monitor Spanish movement in the area. When the botanist Alcide d'Orbigny stopped at Barra in 1830, he noted that its three thousand or so tattered inhabitants traded in everything the region had to offer: dried fish, sarsaparilla, Brazil nuts, turtle-egg oil.

The development of a technique to cure latex changed everything.

Growing demand for rubber prompted Brazil to internationalize the Amazon in 1867, but the days of Michelins, Dunlops and Goodyears were still years away. Another decade elapsed before the first freighter dropped anchor at Manaus. After that, however, there was no stopping them.

Harvesting wild rubber

A *seringueiro*, or tapper, made the rounds of his marked trees by following a trail that defined his reserved harvesting zone. To turn a profit, every day he had to 'milk' his hundred trees (opposite) within the first four hours in the morning, before the sun thickened the sap and sealed off the wound. Another round of the trees to collect the latex (total daily yield: about five or six kilos), and then it was back to his shack to cure the harvest, smoking it over a smouldering fire of green, acid-rich palm nuts. The liquid latex coagulated on a twirled paddle (left), eventually building up to a thirty- or forty-kilo *pele*, or ball of rubber. This chore behind him, he went back into the forest to gather palm nuts for the next day's curing. Only then did he take time from his work to eat and steal a little rest.

A vicious circle

When the rainy season made tapping impracticable, the *seringueiro* floated his harvest downriver to Manaus, where his *aviador* would be waiting for him (opposite). Once the *peles* were split, graded (above) and weighed (below), this middleman signed a new contract with his client – but only after deducting his earnings from his running tab of trade goods. The *aviador*'s warehouses were crammed with tinned foods, beverages, clothing and everything a wretched tapper could develop a craving for during his lonely months in the rain forest. Small wonder that a *seringueiro* invariably left owing his *aviador* more than when he came. Year after year the tapper who fancied himself 'free' simply added yet another link to the chain of debt bondage between himself and his pitiless master.

Manaus was built up under Dr Ribeiro, who became state governor in 1893. 'I found a village and turned it into a modern city,' he reportedly once declared. When the first electric trams (below) began running, three theatrical companies were performing at the newly opened Opera House (left). The city also boasted three hospitals, including one for Portuguese people and one for the insane. Home to ten private secondary schools, more than twenty-five primary schools and a public library, it professed propriety and fostered science.

Rubber was now an exportable commodity. In 1850 Barra was made a provincial capital, renamed Manaus and allocated its first government funds. That year, it shipped nearly one thousand tons of rubber to Pará. The figure jumped to three thousand by 1870, twelve thousand by 1880 and twenty thousand by the turn of the century.

Manaus burgeoned into a metropolis of fifty thousand inhabitants. Tatters gave way to attire purchased, if not actually laundered, in London and Paris. Business was transacted not in *milreis* notes, but in gold coins, and not on the ramshackle tables of olden days, but in big, smart cafés where champagne, whiskey and cognac were served by specially trained staff brought in from Europe. Freighters chugged toward New York and Liverpool laden with rubber; they returned full of bankers and pretty women. In short, life on the Amazon was no longer dull.

When the city began to sprawl over marshland, Portuguese paving stones (and the pavers to lay them) were shipped in from Lisbon. Electric trams clattered along its sixteen km of avenues at a time when Bostonians had to make do with horsecars. Every morning, telephone subscribers – there were three hundred when the first lines were installed in 1897 – called major stock exchanges all over the world to fix the price of rubber. High above the roofs of the city rose the green, yellow and blue dome of the Opera

'In Amazonia there is a universal love of trade,' Alfred Russel Wallace wrote in 1889. 'We find the province [of Pará] overrun with traders, the greater part of whom deserve no better name than peddlers, only they carry their goods in a canoe instead of upon their backs.' Fifty years later freighters crammed with such goods emptied their holds into huge warehouses, and businessmen prospered.

House, a lavish embodiment of Manaus' golden age.

Created expressly for transatlantic service, the Booth Line inaugurated regular steamship runs between Manaus and Liverpool that same year. The city had truly arrived.

Boom to bust

Between 1908 and 1910, when Manaus was at the zenith of its power, eighty million rubber trees spread over some 3 million square kilometres of forest were under development. Manaus was exporting eighty thousand tons of raw rubber annually; export duties alone were covering 40 per cent of Brazil's national debt. But the days of the boom were soon over. Seeds smuggled out of Amazonia thirty years earlier had grown into the vast rubber plantations of Malaysia, which would outstrip all competition in terms of yield and production costs. Moreover, trees exhausted by years of relentless tapping were producing a little less latex each year. Amazonia was now on a collision course with financial upheaval.

In the late 19th century the port of Manaus (above) offered all the luxuries a visitor could require – including first-class passage on the Amazon.

People started declaring bankruptcy. By 1912 they were selling off their assets at a loss. Empires built as if by magic collapsed like houses of cards. The Opera House closed its doors; nightclubs and luxury shops were shuttered. The only places doing steady business were auction houses, where onetime tycoons divested themselves of jewelry, furniture and artwork. Notices at Booth Line ticket windows announced that all sailings bound for Europe were booked months in advance. One thing did not change: the timeless indifference of the poor, confined to outlying districts where fat women lazed on thatched-palm verandas while knots of children scampered about barefoot, kicking up dust that turned them red wherever asphalt roads narrowed and peetered out into dirt tracks, snaking through the dark green jungle.

Yet in that very same year, a railway stretching 350 kilometres from Madeira to Mamoré was inaugurated some two thousand kilometres away.

'Mad Maria' – that was what engineers nicknamed the colossal, genocidal Madeira-Mamoré Railway project. Europeans calculated the cost of the railways they built in their African colonies in human lives per sleeper. By that standard, this was the costliest railway of them all. Construction began in 1908 in a particularly remote, densely forested and disease-ridden area of Brazil and Bolivia. Everything had to be brought in from all over the world by ship, mules and porters: charcoal from Wales, steel from Pittsburgh and, ironically, wood from Australia because only termite-resistant eucalyptus wood would do for the sleepers. The railway was supposed to have opened the huge rubber reserves of Acre and Madre de Diós to the outside world. But by the time it was finished, five years later, the rubber market had collapsed. Six thousand labourers had perished for nothing.

Its purpose: to create an easier transport route from Bolivia to Pôrto Velho, Brazil, which could be reached by freighters on the Amazon. Slicing through the rain forest, this railway cost an enormous amount of money, took five years to build and claimed six thousand lives. It was to prove useless: Bolivian rubber was too expensive.

Suárez of Bolivia: the Rockefeller of rubber

A truly self-made man, Suárez had started out barefoot and become the richest rubber baron in Amazonia. His assets included about 8 million hectares in Bolivia, two townships (Riberalta and Villa Bella) on the Beni River, a whole relay system of Suárez and Brothers mooring stations for his own fleet of boats, and exclusive shipping rights on the Madeira. Originally there were seven Suárez brothers, but one of them was killed when he led a company police force into Caripuna territory. Three hundred Caripuna Indians were slaughtered for one Suárez.

The Suárezes claimed that these Indians were poor workers; they were lazy, like all the rest, and they were hard to recruit. A friend of theirs on the Madre de Diós River hit upon a novel solution. He rounded up six hundred

The man sporting this stylish moustache would not have looked out of place at a European spa. Rubber baron Suárez emanated the unobtrusive respectability of the truly rich. When his wife died, he built a monument to her in the heart of the rain forest, at Cachoeira Esperanza, above the magnificent falls of the same Madeira River that had witnessed the start of his fortune.

Indian slave girls for breeding purposes and placed his harem at the disposal of his guests. Then all he had to do was wait for their offspring to grow until they were big enough to work.

Arana: a gentleman of dubious respectability

Far less boorish than Suárez, Julio Arana impressed the ladies as being a civilized man, olive complexion notwithstanding. People would talk about his library, his house in London, his children's real English nanny, his predilection for family life. But not much else. Arana was an unobtrusive man, a foil for his nightclub-hopping brothers. Every morning at the same time, he would stride into the offices of the Peruvian Amazon Company – his lifework – and stay cooped up there for the whole day.

A shrewd, far-sighted strategist, he knew that Bolivian rubber, the cornerstone of his wealth, was too far away from the marketplace. That is why he backed the proposed Madeira-Mamoré railway.

With busy boat traffic, exports of Amazonian rubber quickly skyrocketed and consumer prices rose at breakneck speed. In 1900 a chicken at Manaus cost the equivalent of £15, and a bunch of carrots £5 – but the rich grew richer and colonial life burgeoned.

" RED RUBBER " ONCE MORE :

On 20 July 1912 *The Illustrated London News* ran a two-page article on 'The Putumayo Revelations'; the headline read '30,000 Lives: 4,000 Tons'. The photographs revealed conditions in Julio Arana's Indian camps and showed how, for example, the overseers in the La Chorrera and El Encanto camps beat the Indians' legs with tapir-hide whips that left disfiguring pads of scar tissue.

That is also why he started seizing 30,000 square kilometres of forest further north, along the Putumayo. The area was rich in wild rubber trees, deep in a disputed area between Colombia and Peru, and much closer to Manaus. This was also the homeland of the Bora, the Andoke, the Huitoto, the Ocaina – peaceable Indian tribes known since the days of the conquistadors – some fifty thousand people in all.

Arana recruited a private militia of black men from Barbados, subjects of Her Britannic Majesty. And he had the clever idea of setting up headquarters in London and arranging for City financiers to

THE PUTUMAYO REVELATIONS.

From El Encanto ('Enchantment') camp to *Arbeit Macht Frei* – the motto above the gates of Auschwitz and Buchenwald – the same torturer's humour is exhibited. In this respect, Julio Arana was ahead of his time.

underwrite his firm. That gave it an air of respectability. The sacrosanct militiamen were armed with Winchesters and sent into the jungle to recruit Indians. They rounded up thirty thousand and confined them to company-owned villages.

The disgrace of the Peruvian Amazon Company

Soon, however, rumours started circulating in London. The treatment of native workers left something to be desired. The City's good name was called into question; public opinion was roused. Five years later a court of inquiry issued a report revealing that the rain forest had been turned into a killing field. All but eight thousand of the fifty thousand Indians in the region had been killed. Each ton of rubber had cost seven human lives.

"It is my wish that nothing My Lord the King, my daughter the Princess and my son the Prince may do, or allow to be done, shall bring any harm to the Indians living either on islands or *terra firma*, to either their persons or property. Indeed, they shall see to it that these peoples are treated in a just and kindly fashion."

Last Will of Queen Isabella of Spain

CHAPTER 5

THE INDIAN AND THE RAIN FOREST

Native people (Puri Indians, left) and animals (an 1820 lithograph of an iguana, right) lived as one with the rain forest.

It is hard to be objective about an inscrutable world whose inhabitants have an outlook so different from our own. The problem between the Indians and us is one of culture. We have given priority to a culture that evolves by working against nature. We think in terms of coercion and conflict: nature must be subdued. As we see it, having takes precedence over being.

Indian culture, unlike ours, is a process of accommodation to nature. Animals are people like us, the Indians say; trees and mountains have one or more spirits. Indians scrounge, pilfer and kill, too, if need be – none of which goes against the laws of nature – but they never hoard. Ecology, ever-present, is woven seamlessly into the fabric of their lives.

The quiet partnership of Indian and nature

An Indian's superbly carved and balanced canoe skims the river surface without a ripple. As he trots along his network of practically invisible forest trails, he is careful not to make the slightest sound lest he startle the enemy. Then, whether stalking other Indians or herds of peccaries – killing only what he needs – he suddenly barks as loudly as the packs of hounds that live among certain tribes. In a twinkling, everything falls silent again.

It is common for Indians to hunt with the bow, and they have an endless variety of interchangeable, 'customized' arrowheads from which to choose. Lance-shaped points of bamboo, hardened in fire to produce razor-sharp edges, tip arrows designed for use in battle. (The Yanomami also use them to cut their hair.) Feathers are such an important part of body adornment that Indians use special blunted tips, like those on fencing foils, to stun birds and leave the prized plumage undamaged. But their most sophisticated weapon remains the blowgun, fashioned from a smoothed and polished hollow cane. A single puff can shoot a dart the size of a big needle into a target more than twenty metres away. Although an inch deep, the wound would be slight were the tip not coated with curare, that subtle poison that kills quietly by gradually paralyzing smooth muscle tissue. Bows and arrows are often two metres long, spears three metres, and blowguns about four. Perhaps the most surprising thing of all is that the Indians are so adept at handling such long weapons in the heart of the densest jungle.

"The warlike relations of the whites with most Indian tribes have contributed greatly to the multiplicity of references to weapons from the earliest chroniclers to our own day. In many cases weapons are the only aspects of native culture known to us. Travellers have always shown a particular interest in weapons."
Alfred Métraux

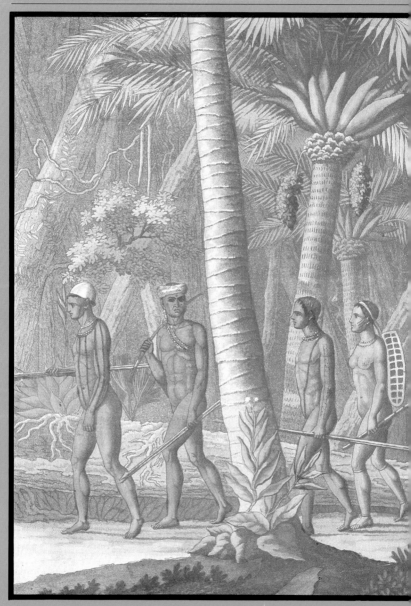

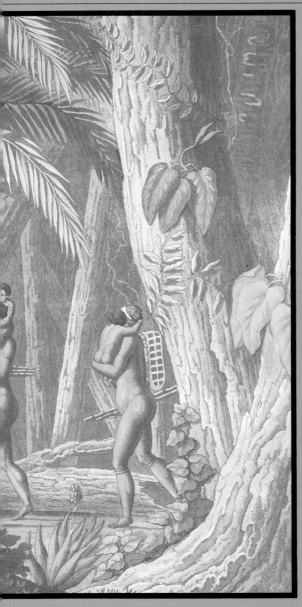

Learning how to walk

The Botocudo Indians (left) demonstrate a point that ethnologist Pierre Clastres learned when he asked his hosts, the Aché, to escort him through the forest. They balked. 'Their greatest fear was that I might slow them down. Finally, they agreed to go with me, and I quickly realized that their misgivings were well-founded.' He was expected to 'make a beeline and not waste time. They walked at a brisk clip, and I'd find myself bringing up the rear, impeded if not immobilized by lianas I kept tripping over or by others that would suddenly lash me to a tree trunk. I'd snag my clothes on thorns and make frantic efforts to shake them loose. Not only was I lagging behind, but making a commotion! The Aché, however, were silent, supple, efficient. Before long, it dawned on me that one of the things holding me back was my clothing. Branches and lianas glanced harmlessly off bare Indian skin. I decided to do as they did and shed my clothes.'

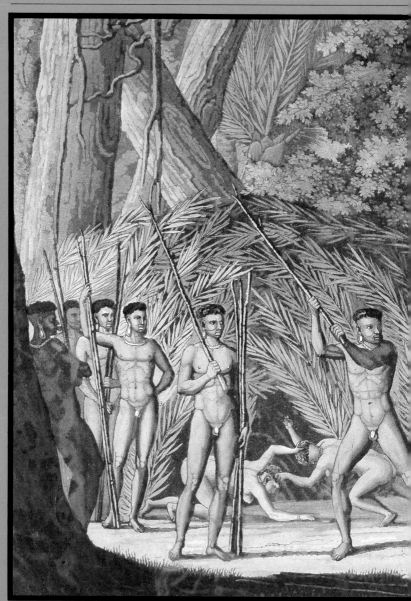

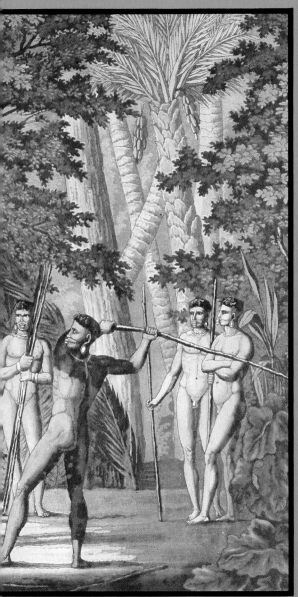

Bacteriological warfare

Two major tributaries of the Amazon, the Juruá and the Purús, flow through the Brazilian state of Acre, which borders Peru and Bolivia. Since they are navigable along their entire lengths, upriver journeys to their headwaters date back to the early 19th century. The Indians who once inhabited this region welcomed explorers peaceably. Everything changed with the rubber boom, because the area proved to be exceptionally rich in wild rubber trees. Suárez began building his empire – on the misfortune of Indians. To weed them out as expeditiously as possible, *seringueiros* (prospectors) resorted to techniques the English and French had successfully tried out on North American Indians in the 18th century. They would even hand out disease-infected clothing. Today virtually nothing remains of these peoples.

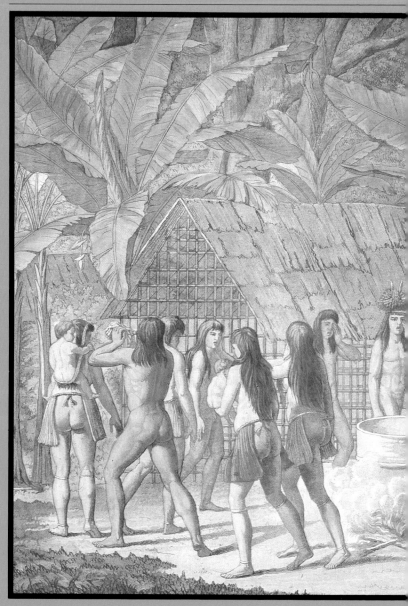

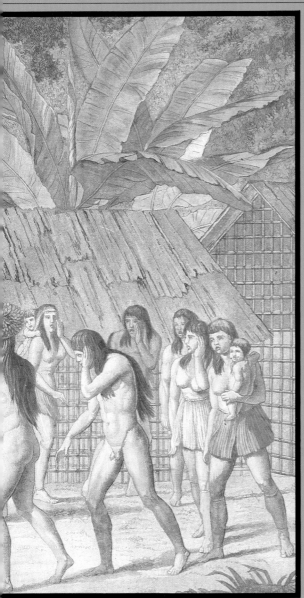

Dancing

Like people all over the world, Indians (left, the Camacan) consider dancing both language and celebration, a throwback to a time when there was no clear dividing line between the sacred and the profane. Older than speech (witness the mating dances of birds), dancing transcends speech, for it conveys what words cannot. Now stately, now frenzied, dancing expresses the life instinct whenever it sweeps aside dualities – body and soul, visible and unseen – and makes existence whole again, in an ecstasy beyond time. Certainly countless, often ceremonious, occasionally freewheeling, Indian dances punctuate all of life's events, from the momentous to the pedestrian: birth, puberty, death, war, marriage, building a house, starting a garden.

An Amazonian invention: the barbecue

During the dry season, when rivers are at their lowest, the Indians build dams of braided reeds; farther upstream they crush bundles of herbs in the water. The drugged fish rise to the surface and drift down with the current to the dam, where the Indians scoop them up by the basketful. This is known as '*barbasco* fishing', from the name of the plant they use. The next stage was the invention of long, raised softwood racks for roasting and smoking the catch over hot coals. The cured fish would then be ready for storage during the rainy season, when game is scarce. Peccaries and tapirs taken during hunts would be butchered and dressed in the same fashion.

The Indians of Haiti called this rack a *barbacoa*, and the Spanish borrowed the term from them. Thus, the modern barbecue is a good deal more American than people suspect.

A magical world, the supernatural omnipresent

'The Amazonian Indian is apt to sense the presence of supernatural beings in any natural sight that strikes him as strange or awe-inspiring,' Alfred Métraux

Barbecuing a tapir (below).

At a time when the Indian community is besieged by the outside world in ways that threaten its very existence, the continuing presence of the shaman is the surest guarantee of group cohesiveness and, therefore, survival – something both ethnologists and missionaries have had to acknowledge. Diviner, priest and healer rolled into one, a shaman watches over the health of individuals and is consulted in all matters involving the welfare of his people.

writes. 'Waterfalls, certain eddies in the river, oddly shaped rocks are the dwelling-places of cantankerous spirits that bear close watching and must be appeased.'

But one cannot ferret out the supernatural unless one knows how to cross over from the visible to the invisible world. Enter the shaman, the guide of souls, who can take leave of his body and go off in search of spirits that have been driven away by illness. He also assists his entire people with the difficult transitions in life of birth, death and puberty, for which certain nations prescribe dangerous initiation rites involving copious drink-offerings, tobacco and hallucinogenic or psychedelic drugs. The shaman's expertise in narcotics, acquired during a very long and perilous apprenticeship, enables him to guide the community towards collective ecstasy and to ensure that rituals allowing a safe return to the here and now are properly observed. Some drugs are smoked, others ingested as decoctions, inhaled as snuff, even taken as

Hallucinations and trances are not the prerogatives of shamans. Shared by all, drugs are an adjunct to social gatherings. For example, it is customary for members of the Ouitoto and Yanomami tribes to blow narcotic snuff into one another's nostrils. At such times, drugs not only become a form of property exchange in accordance with the tribe's moral code, but help to liberate the group and promote its psychic well-being in the face of all the evil forces besieging it. This is where psychedelic drugs come in, complementing hallucinogens; contact with the supernatural need not be a fearful, deadly serious affair.

enemas. Yanomami hunters use *ebene* snuff on a daily basis to sharpen their senses. Elsewhere, the *yopo* found among the Piaroa and most peoples in the region is as famous as their curare and, like it, exchanged during gift-giving ceremonies.

Birds and feathers: colourful, rich adornment

Playful, imaginative, appearance-conscious, Indians enjoy showing off in front of their peers. Even more than women, men carefully adorn their bodies with skillful designs in red paint from annatto seeds, with occasional highlights in carbon black and blue vegetable dye. Facial designs are in black, red and white, sometimes given a glossy finish; more intricate and delicate patterns are the rule for women. This gaudy attire is enhanced by many kinds of finery: ear ornaments tipped with long tufts of toucan feathers, large tooth necklaces (proof of a hunter's ability), seed chains, braided-hair ligatures to make arm and leg muscles bulge, lip disks, pectorals, pendants. Palm skirts and feathered crowns or diadems are saved for

ritual celebrations. On these occasions, the men form solemn processions and display a sharpened bludgeon now used solely for ceremonial purposes, but which Tupi and Carib Indians, among others, once used to execute prisoners during cannibalistic rituals.

The opening of a communal house is an occasion for festivity, with several days of ritual intoxication

The communal house is a fundamental symbol. Spacious enough to accommodate a hundred people, it serves as a kind of village square, usually roofed, with living quarters fanning out from the centre. It embodies the basic unit of Indian society, which is not the couple, much less the individual, but the kinship group. Depending on age, everyone in a communal house is someone else's child or parent, although couples and their offspring are acknowledged and respected as such. However, several extended families can live together under the same roof. The communal house is also a symbolic representation of their cosmos and cosmogony. It is the one 'book' that everyone must learn to read.

The tract of cleared land between the village and the surrounding forest is planted with manioc – a source of bread and wine – banana trees, and occasionally a few stalks of sugarcane, pineapple or papaya. A few years later, once the rains have damaged the roof of the house and washed away the shallow layer of topsoil, the fields are left fallow, and the group moves on to another location, clears the land once again, and

A Curuchu Indian communal house, as depicted in an 18th-century Portuguese drawing (below).

The Tukuna of the Río Solimões (left), a sizable Indian nation at the crossroads of Brazil, Colombia and Peru, managed to stay on good terms with their white neighbours for two centuries without compromising their sociocultural integrity. However, according to recent reports in the international press, they have become the victims of murderous assaults in Brazil.

builds another communal house. A fresh round of celebration then begins.

The Yanomami can slip through the densest jungles

The Yanomami Indians, whose territory straddles the border of Venezuela and Brazil, probably represent the earliest surviving stage of Indian culture. Perpetually on the move, they lived until recently in complete and unrivalled symbiosis with nature. A Yanomami man would carry nothing but a bow, three arrows longer than he is tall, and a bludgeon fashioned from half a bow. He would keep a few spare arrowheads and a pencil-sized stick with an agouti-tooth tip in a small bamboo quiver that hung down his back.

The Yanomami, basically warriors, live by hunting and gathering and by limited cultivation of native fruit trees. (They scrounge, pilfer, raid beehives and even catch armadillos in their burrows.) Their diet is rudimentary and, except for meat, their food is usually eaten raw. They sleep curled up in small hammocks put together from bark strips.

Various types of shelters used by Indians in the Brazilian Amazon.

"Ocelot Spirit, come down into me! *Hekura*, you did not help me. For whole nights I pondered my vengeance. I saw the Vulture Spirit and the Moon Spirit. Moon Spirit was struck by Suhirina's arrow when he invaded the dwelling, eager for human flesh; and from his wound, from his spilled blood, were born a multitude of flesh-eating vultures. Moon Spirit, Vulture Spirit, you are cannibals. Vulture, your head is polluted with blood, your nostrils teem with worms. The dragonflies gather in the sky. Omawe pierced the earth with his bow; out of the hole he made spring a gusher of water that reached the sky and formed a canopy. Up there the dragonflies multiply; up there live the thirsty ones! Let them come down into me! Omawe has burned my tongue! Let them moisten my tongue and refresh it! Those who have ordered the demons to capture our children will receive my vengeance, wherever they may be."

Yanomami shaman's curse on the death of a child, as recorded by Jacques Lizot

Their lives are intertwined with the overwhelmingly lush – and haunted – world around them.

The largest tribe of unacculturated people in South America is struggling to survive

Could there be a connection between what was only recently the very large number of Yanomami and the fact that they managed to avoid all contact with white people until modern times? It would seem so, teetering as they are now between well-being and endangerment. At any rate, we know for certain that the Yanomami people were still flourishing until only a very few years ago. But they were not living in total isolation. In Venezuela, the Yanomami material culture was evolving – but without borrowing from the 'white world'. Over the past quarter of a century, they have been adopting certain advances – canoes, woven cotton hammocks, small banana and manioc groves – probably as a result of interaction with the Yekuana, a tribe of sedentary farmers. The two peoples, weary of feuding, have been exchanging more than traditions; they are even intermarrying. This transformation might have proceeded smoothly had it

About half the size of France, Yanomami territory was until recently the last undisturbed sanctuary in Amazonia. The earliest peaceful contacts with Yanomami groups date from the Orinoco-Amazon expedition of 1949-50 (in which the author participated). They were then considered fearsome, legendary beings; the Yanomami, for their part, looked upon whites as dangerous, man-eating spirits. Scientific scrutiny of the Yanomami began in the 1960s.

The chances are that the Yanomami would have gone on living in another world, as they always had, if Brazilian prospectors had not stumbled upon mammoth gold and diamond deposits on the Amazon slope of Sierra Parima. Thus, El Dorado was reborn at the very spot where the famous adventurer and inmate of the Tower of London, Sir Walter Raleigh, thought he would find it four hundred years ago. Starting in 1987, this gold rush brought forty thousand people – and their culture and diseases – into Yanomami lands.

not been for the intrusion of white people looking for gold and diamonds.

Once again, Amazonia is being overrun by treasure hunters

The latest gold rush, which began in 1987, brought prospectors, *garimpeiros* – a pickaxe in one hand and a Winchester in the other – into the jungle to seek their fortunes. About 40,000 people flooded Yanomami territory in Brazil alone, with estimates of the jackpot reaching more than £500 million a year.

Curiously, history repeated itself in the Space Age as hordes of hungry, penniless fortune-seekers trudged toward Sierra Parima to scale a hitherto undisturbed mountain in search of gold. In May 1988 the London-based tribal defence movement Survival International sounded the alarm: 'Today the Yanomami Indians are facing the most serious threat to their survival ever. Twenty thousand miners have overrun their territory in the last month alone.'

The implications of such an influx of people have been vast. The delicate balance between people and nature has been upset, and the Yanomami are paying the price. Diseases brought by miners – malaria, tuberculosis, venereal disease – have killed at least fifteen hundred Brazilian Yanomami. In 1990 *Time* magazine quoted one Yanomami man as saying,

'They gave us rice and wheat, but then we got sick. They pretended to be our friends, but they are killing us.'

As word of the crisis spread, a huge outcry in support of the Yanomami built up, and within a few years the Brazilian government was engaged in a massive effort to eject the prospectors from Yanomami lands and to set the land aside for the Yanomami alone. In April 1991 Brazilian president Fernando Collor de Mello issued a number of decrees reserving a huge swath of land for the Indians and prohibiting others from entering. On the other hand, though, the reserve has been divided into many sections separated by zones in which the *garimpeiros* and other treasure hunters circulate freely, disturbing the Yanomami. What is more, the parcelling of their territory has undermined the Yanomami's ability to hunt and gather successfully.

But even if the Yanomami and other Indian tribes survive the threats to their health and to their culture, the impact of the white invasion is indelible. Change is inevitable; the Yanomami will never be the same. 'The question is,' says Venezuelan anthropologist Roberto Lizaraldi, 'whether it will be on their terms or someone else's.'

Covering an area in eastern Amazonia equal to England and France combined, the iron mine and associated development projects collectively known as Grande Carajas are aimed at catapulting Brazil to world power status.

Backed up by the very latest in technology, the latter-day invaders are broadening their field of operations over the whole of the Amazon basin, from its very heart to its outermost reaches. Prospecting for minerals – not to mention unprecedented quantities of precious stones and metals – has turned up fresh deposits of iron, coal, oil, bauxite, uranium, copper and lead, inviting development by big business.

Every day more of the rain forest goes up in smoke

Like its inhabitants, the rain forest itself is threatened from all sides by mining activity, by intensive

A string of dams provides hydro-electric power for Grande Carajas and a massive agricultural programme. Some thirteen thousand Indians used to call this region home. For them progress translates into an all-too-familiar aftermath: epidemics and pollution introduced by whites, deforestation of traditional hunting grounds and social disintegration.

cultivation of nutrient-poor soils sucked dry by modern farmers large and small, by logging.

However, it is not so much big business (when managed efficiently) that is responsible for the appalling deforestation currently underway throughout the whole Amazon basin; rather, it is traditional farmers. Slash-and-burn farming, which causes little damage when sporadic and confined to very small patches of forest (the Indian practice), hastens widespread soil degradation and erosion.

Pollution has taken its toll on the Pirarucu, the giant fish of Amazonia

Development has affected the flow of water in the Amazon basin, which not only serves as an irreplaceable transportation network but also provides indigenous communities with fish to supplement the animal protein otherwise limited to what they can catch by hunting in the forest. Across much of the Amazon proper, the growing number of gigantic dams and the rapidly escalating pollution of major

Large-scale industry is not the only source of water pollution. Gold miners use mercury to recover the precious metal and foul the river with its poisonous residue.

rivers have already all but wiped out the huge, but harmless, pirarucu, once a staple of the region because it often weighs two hundred kilos. In the early 20th century trade in dried or salted pirarucu was still such that it was commonly referred to as the freshwater cod.

Upriver, in mountain streams, the mercury used by gold miners has killed off fish along hundreds of kilometres of river; in some regions game is scarce and the soil so poor that manioc roots do not weigh a quarter of what they do elsewhere. Thus, yet another scourge – malnutrition – is taking a toll on village populations.

A number of dams have been built indiscriminately, flooding preserves once inhabited by thousands of surviving Indians for the sake of producing what some say are negligible amounts of energy.

Indians: a raw material ruthlessly exploited by tour operators

In some cases the Indians themselves – especially if they sport feathers on their heads – become a resource that can be developed, and fall prey to tour operators who prod them into degrading 'reenactments' of their own lives. This undermines the distinct identity of these peoples whose perfectly balanced relationship with their environment has led more than a few admiring observers to conclude that, apart from occasional cannibalism, it is they who are civilized and we who are the savages.

Traditional ways of life are threatened by development. The huge pirarucu, once an Amazonian staple, is now found in only limited numbers.

A living legend as a peacemaker and staunch defender of Indians, Colonel Rondon began his military career at the age of sixteen as an army private. In 1910 he founded the Indian Protection Service in the name of the positivist ideal emblazoned on the Brazilian flag. It was the first government agency of its kind in the Western Hemisphere.

Utopian dreaming, some will say. Very well, then, let us speak realistically. Over the years a highly placed Brazilian official has unabashedly stated that, humanism or no, Indians would never stand in the way of development. The current population of Brazil stands at 153.8 million, but some experts predict that the figure will rise to 200, then 300, and eventually 500 million. In light of such forecasts, 200,000 Indians in the forest do not seem to count for very much.

Indians discussing Indians

The threat has not gone unheeded, and a new trend is emerging as the century draws to a close. Some Indian peoples (most Indians in the temperate areas of the Andean Cordillera, long accustomed to living near whites, and several large ethnic groups in the southern part of Brazilian Amazonia) have realized that they had better work out a defence strategy based on not just bows and arrows – although that can sometimes prove a powerful deterrent – but on opening up a dialogue with the whites, using their language and learning to work within their system.

They have banded together in associations and armed themselves with constitutionally recognized

rights. Their mission is to safeguard their material and spiritual heritage. This is clearly the most significant turn of events that can be identified as we approach the 21st century.

The problem of initiating a dialogue between two worlds

At the beginning of this century Indians had no constitutional rights in any republic along the Amazon, but the rubber scandal finally compelled the Brazilian government to create the Indian Protection Service in 1910. The first agency of its kind, it was designed to protect Indians from starvation, poverty, exploitation by whites and the diseases they introduced. Its architect and guiding light, Colonel Cândido Mariano da Silva Rondon, a native Brazilian, was so popular that he was promoted to

Rondon escorted Theodore Roosevelt on a scientific expedition to Amazonia in 1913 and 1914. Roosevelt called him a 'gallant officer, a high-minded gentleman, and an intrepid explorer'.

the rank of marshal a few years before his death in 1956 at the age of ninety. The watchword he bequeathed to Indian Protection Service agents – 'Die if necessary, but never kill' – vanished with him. Created in all innocence as an agency of the Ministry of Agriculture, the service became mired in a series of scandals from which it never recovered. By executive order, it was superseded in 1972 by FUNAI (Fundaçao Nacional do Indio) and its operations placed under the jurisdiction of the Ministry of the Interior. That was a step in the right direction.

Most Amazonian countries have followed Brazil's lead. They have set up government agencies within their interior ministries to oversee Indian affairs, although within very different legislative parameters. Some recognize Indians as full-fledged nationals who enjoy the same rights and responsibilities as their fellow-citizens. Others – including Brazil, home to half of all Amazonian Indians – regard them as *de*

"The social structure, languages, beliefs and traditions of Indians are hereby recognized, as are their natural rights to lands they have traditionally occupied. Water utilization, prospecting and development of mineral resources may not be undertaken on indigenous lands unless authorized by the National Congress and after consultation with the affected communities. Lands traditionally occupied by Indians are inalienable, and the rights pertaining thereto indefeasible."
  Article 266, New Constitution of Brazil June 1988

facto minors who do not have the right to vote and whose rights have to be mediated through their caretaker agency, FUNAI.

A big step forward, provided Brazil enforces its own laws

The constitution of June 1988 made no provision for Indian suffrage, an issue that has sparked controversy in Brazil among self-proclaimed champions of the Indian cause. Some denounce the omission as paternalistic. Others argue that the government cannot grant rights to those Indians who are more acclimatized to white culture and – a key distinction – who speak Portuguese, and at the same time withhold them from those who choose to stay in the forest. And they feel that all Indians have a right to equal protection against the unscrupulous adventurers always poised to plunder their lands.

What the new Brazilian constitution does recognize – not an inconsiderable concession – is the Indians' right to lands they have traditionally occupied and exclusive rights to profits generated by underground resources. However, Congress still has the authority to grant or deny companies permission to develop those resources.

Thus, throughout most of the Amazon region, organizers of Indian self-help groups are aware that the fundamental rights of their peoples to land, language and culture have been unanimously recognized, at least on paper. As representatives of their interests, they must struggle to bridge the often considerable gap between law and enforcement, and to see to it that these lofty principles do not evaporate in the tropical air.

Are forest-dwelling Indians doomed to extinction?

Mutual-aid associations have sprung up in Amazonia at all levels of Indian society, from villages to tribes, nations and countries.

The Indians have shown that they can sit down at a negotiating table with whites and push just as hard for their cultural rights as for their language and land, which goes to show (with all due respect to doommongers) that integration with the modern world need not always lead to acculturation, that unfailing destroyer of human individuality. Culture is what cements individual Indians to their group, without which they would cease to exist. As long as they continue to press for these rights, their identity is safe.

Therefore, our reply to those who ask if the Indians are dying out is a fairly resounding 'no' if they mean those peoples with representation, some of whom are still forest-dwellers and have only sporadic contact with the outside world. This includes fully half of the 800 to 900,000 Indians who live in Amazonia proper. But what about the rest?

Planners of highways across Amazonia paid little heed to the socio-cultural balances they were bound to disturb. Beneath its apparent uniformity, Amazonia is divided into hunting, gathering and tribal migration zones that have evolved over the centuries.

After five hundred years, will the saga of the Amazon end with the murder of El Dorado?

Global awareness of the problems in Amazonia has created the beginnings of change. With international

efforts to preserve the rain forests ('the earth's lungs') and its denizens gaining momentum, hope lies on the horizon. Deforestation and pollution are being fought both locally and on the global scale, and innovative programmes such as 'debt for nature' swaps – in which industrialized countries are relieving debtor nations of some financial burden in exchange for local environmental protection programmes and the creation of new preserves – are exploring new ground. Such efforts, however, will represent real hope for the future only if local authorities enforce the principles of ecology and preservation of indigenous people on all administrative levels. It must also be said that, under the pretext of patrolling the borders and preventing guerrilla movement and drug trafficking, the armed forces stationed in the Amazon frequently abuse their power and they, too, prey on the environment and the Indian communities.

The 1979 words of Darcy Ribeiro, Brazilian anthropologist and political activist, still resound: 'I have failed to reach my goal as an anthropologist: to rescue the Indians of Brazil. That's right, simply rescue them. That is what I've spent the last thirty years trying to do. I have failed. I wanted to rescue them from the atrocities that have spelled extermination for so many Indian peoples.... Rescue them from the resentment and dejection sown in their villages by missionaries, official protectors, scientists, and most of all the landowners who in countless ways deprive them of their most basic right: the right to exist and remain as they are.'

What will the future bring? As international attention focuses on preserving the Amazon rain forest and the people and animals who live there, some people see reason to hope that traditional ways of life will not be completely exterminated.

"We are the descendants of a noble people that lived in balance with nature and took care of the great western continent they called home. We have had to endure the wholesale squandering of our land and people."
        Galibi Indian from
                Surinam

Jívaro   *Caqueta*

Putumayo

Marañón

Quito

ECUADOR   *Ucayali*

Amazon

Andean
Cordillera

Pacific
Ocean

PERU

La Condamine   Humboldt   Bonpland

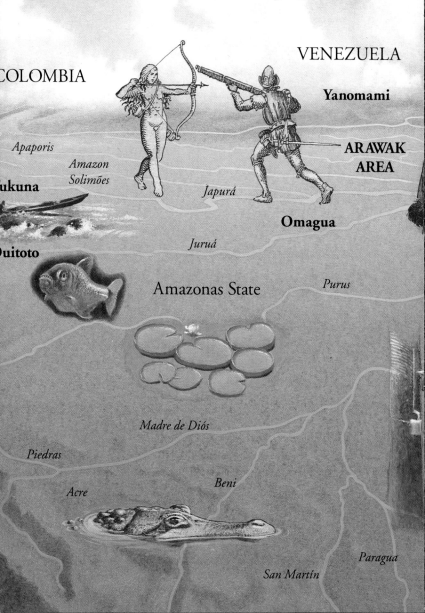

VENEZUELA

COLOMBIA

Yanomami

Apaporis

**ARAWAK
AREA**

*Amazon
Solimões*

ukuna

Japurá

Omagua

uitoto

Juruá

Purus

Amazonas State

Madre de Diós

Piedras

Beni

Acre

Paragua

San Martín

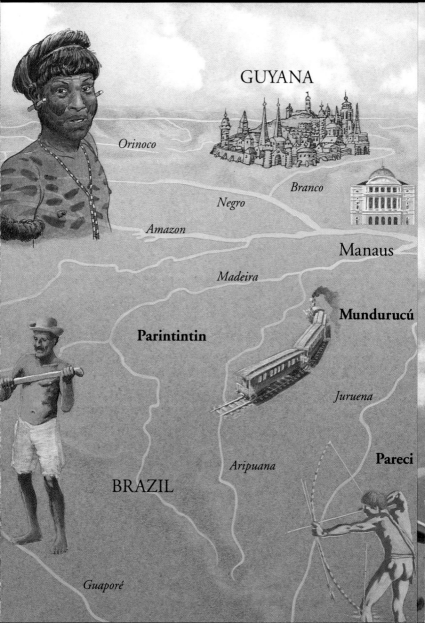

GUYANA

Orinoco

Branco

Negro

Amazon

Manaus

Madeira

Parintintin

Mundurucú

Juruena

Aripuana

Pareci

BRAZIL

Guaporé